Caesar AND ROME

Charlotte Bernard
Art direction by Claude Meunier

A Henry Holt Reference Book
Henry Holt and Company
New York

A PICTURE IS WORTH A THOUSAND WORDS

Xun Zi (313-238 B.C.)

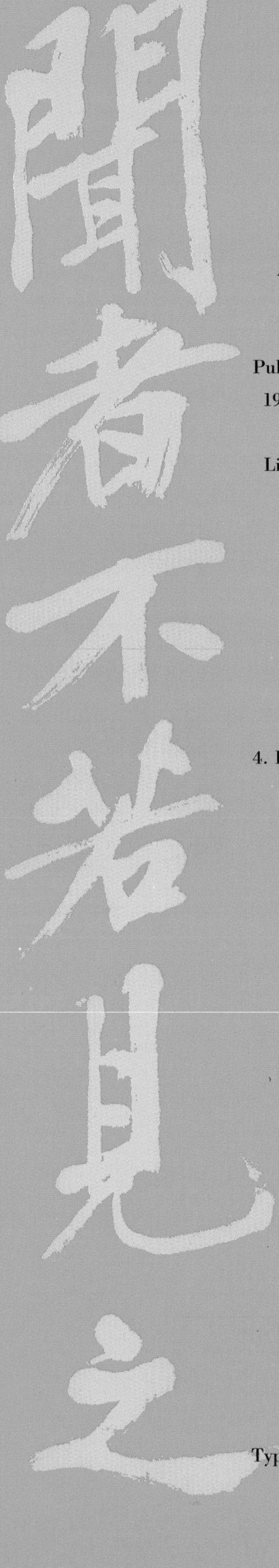

中耀書荀子語录

Henry Holt and Company, Inc.
Publishers since 1866
115 West 18th Street
New York, New York 10011

Published in Canada by Fitzhenry & Whiteside Ltd.,
195 Allstate Parkway, Markham, Ontario L3R 4T8.

Library of Congress Cataloging-in-Publication Data
Bernard, Charlotte.
[César et Rome. English]
Caesar and Rome/Charlotte Bernard.
p. cm.
—(W5 (who, what, where, when, and why) series)
Includes bibliographical references and index.
1. Caesar, Julius. 2. Heads of state—Rome—
Biography. 3. Generals—Rome—Biography.
4. Rome—History—265–30 B.C. I. Title. II. Series.
DG261.B47 1996
937'.05'092—dc20 95-40039
[B] CIP

ISBN 0-8050-4658-5

Henry Holt books are available for special
promotions and premiums.
For details contact: Director, Special Markets.

Originally published in France in 1996 by
Editions Mango under the title *César et Rome*.

First published in the United States in 1996 by
Henry Holt and Company, Inc.

First American Edition—1996

Art direction by Claude Meunier
Idea and series by Dominique Gaussen
American English translation by Vicki Bogard
Typesetting by Jay Hyams and Christopher Hyams Hart

Printed in France
All first editions are printed on acid-free paper.∞
1 2 3 4 5 6 7 8 9 10

CONTENTS

101

B.C.

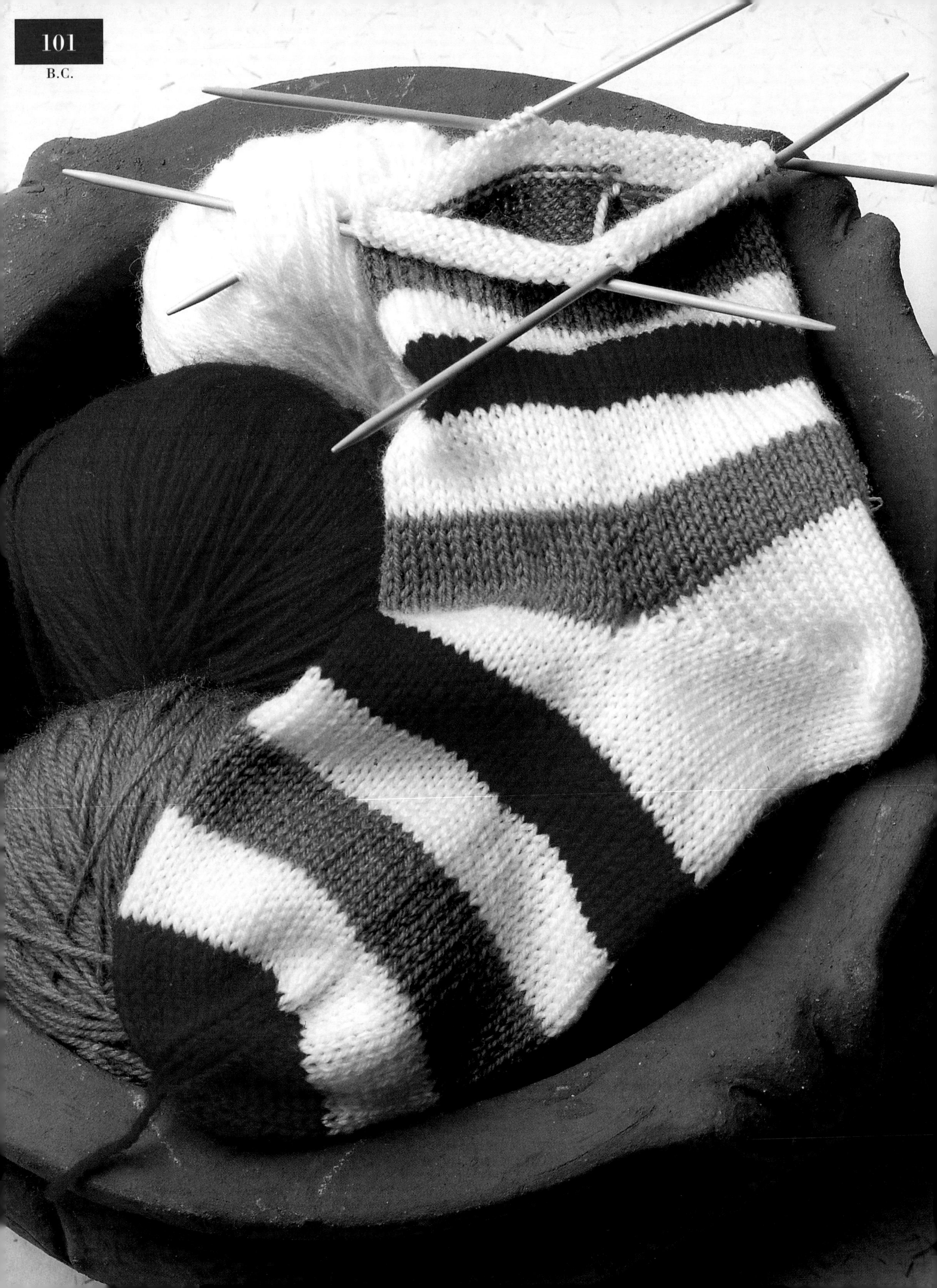

ITALY IS STILL A BOOTIE, BUT ROME IS ALREADY TAKING BIG STEPS

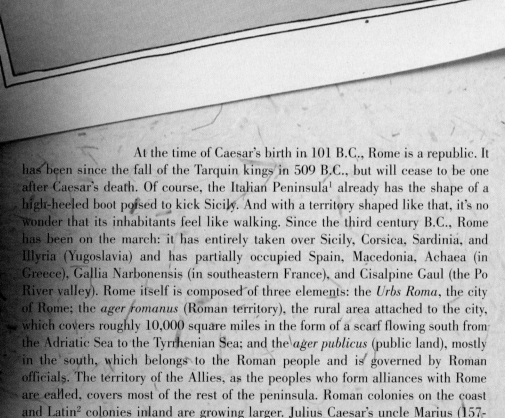

At the time of Caesar's birth in 101 B.C., Rome is a republic. It has been since the fall of the Tarquin kings in 509 B.C., but will cease to be one after Caesar's death. Of course, the Italian Peninsula[1] already has the shape of a high-heeled boot poised to kick Sicily. And with a territory shaped like that, it's no wonder that its inhabitants feel like walking. Since the third century B.C., Rome has been on the march: it has entirely taken over Sicily, Corsica, Sardinia, and Illyria (Yugoslavia) and has partially occupied Spain, Macedonia, Achaea (in Greece), Gallia Narbonensis (in southeastern France), and Cisalpine Gaul (the Po River valley). Rome itself is composed of three elements: the *Urbs Roma*, the city of Rome; the *ager romanus* (Roman territory), the rural area attached to the city, which covers roughly 10,000 square miles in the form of a scarf flowing south from the Adriatic Sea to the Tyrrhenian Sea; and the *ager publicus* (public land), mostly in the south, which belongs to the Roman people and is governed by Roman officials. The territory of the Allies, as the peoples who form alliances with Rome are called, covers most of the rest of the peninsula. Roman colonies on the coast and Latin[2] colonies inland are growing larger. Julius Caesar's uncle Marius (157-86 B.C.) created some of these colonies for veterans[3] to give them land. Italian cities are considered either free or federated, depending on the status Rome gives them when they are conquered. So you can see that Rome is already outgrowing its bootie—and Caesar plans to turn it into one very large boot.

1. Italy designates the central and southern parts of the peninsula (the Itali were a people from the south).
2. These are the original inhabitants of the region of Latium, whose capital is Rome.
3. Former soldiers who had served in the army for about fifteen years.

ALL ROADS LEAD TO ROME
The network of Italian roads dates back mostly to the time of the republic, and each road bears the name of the official who ordered its construction. Roads are usually 13 feet wide, but the closer you get to Rome, the wider the roads become, reaching 30 feet. The Roman via is the ancient equivalent of a highway. It is different from normal roads in that it is very well constructed—four layers of gravel and concrete with a convex surface to help water run off. Such roads usually run in a straight line, regardless of obstacles. The oldest and most famous highway is the Via Appia, or Appian Way, linking Rome to Capua, 310 miles away. Dating back to 312 B.C., it is the first paved road ever built.

For Romans, the known world extends barely past the coasts of the Mediterranean Sea. They visualize their city as the center of an onion, around which are layers of civilized peoples, then the "barbarians," and finally the great unknown—the Ocean. They also use their imaginations to explain the birth of their city: according to legend, the twin brothers Romulus and Remus were abandoned at birth and suckled by a she-wolf. They competed with each other to establish a city on the site of the Palatine Hill where they had been left. Romulus plowed a furrow in the earth to set the boundary of his new city. When Remus entered the city by stepping over the boundary, which was sacred, Romulus killed him. Thus it was Romulus who became the first king of Rome, in 753 B.C.

But Rome in Caesar's time is not just a little garden patch. During the first century B.C. it has almost 1 million inhabitants. (Compare that with Michelangelo's Rome in the sixteenth century, when there are no more than 50,000 inhabitants.)

Let's look at those onion rings in a slightly different way. You have citizens, or freemen, born of fathers who are citizens, and, further out, you have noncitizens, comprised of slaves and freedmen, or former slaves.

The Roman people can be divided into three categories. Patricians come from about one hundred noble families. To be a noble, you have to have an ancestor who held a high government office like consul, praetor, or censor. Plebeians are nonnoble citizens and make up most of the population. Between these two classes are the equites, people from either patrician or plebeian families whose fortune has earned them a high place on the social ladder. The noncitizens form the lowest rank of Roman society. They don't have the right to vote, to serve in the military, or to get married. Most slaves are either prisoners of war or Roman citizens who have been stripped of their civic rights. Slaves can be manumitted—freed from slavery—and thus regain their freedom; owners sometimes give slaves their freedom as a reward for loyal service. Slaves also can buy their freedom. Romans are further divided according to their place of residence into 35 tribes, or administrative districts.

The political system of Rome is an oligarchy, meaning a small number of persons actually rules, in spite of the democratic institutions (the senate and the various *comitia*, or assemblies) in place. Since the social reforming Gracchus brothers (133-121 B.C.), the *populares*, meaning the politicians who support the common people, have gained ground over the *optimates*, the "best men" (they gave themselves the name), meaning the conservative politicians who defend the interests of the patricians.

Surrounding Italy are other civilized peoples. The Egyptians have played a secondary role since the middle of the second century B.C. The Macedonian dynasty has been in power there since 323 B.C. Ptolemy Auletes, father of Cleopatra, has not yet risen to the throne (80-51 B.C.). Farther away but still on the Mediterranean is Greece. Greek expansion has declined since its wars with Rome, which went on for one hundred years, ending in 146 B.C., when the Romans sacked Corinth. Greeks settled in the southern part of the Italian Peninsula and in Sicily in the eighth century B.C., at the height of their colonial expansion. Gaul is made up of about sixty tribes spread out in the different regions: *Cisalpine* Gaul (in the valley of the Po River), which is now part of Italy, divided into *Transpadane* Gaul (north of the Po) and *Cispadane* Gaul (south of the Po), and *Transalpine* Gaul (beyond the Alps). Transalpine Gaul covers the territory of modern France but also includes parts of Italy and Belgium. As for the barbarians, the Teutons (a northern people defeated by the Roman general Marius in 102 B.C. at Aquae Sextiae) and their neighbors the Cimbri (crushed by Marius at Vercellae in 101 B.C.) ravage Gaul between 105 and 102 B.C., thus posing a threat to the Italian Peninsula to the south.

ROME IS ALREADY THE CENTER OF THE WORLD

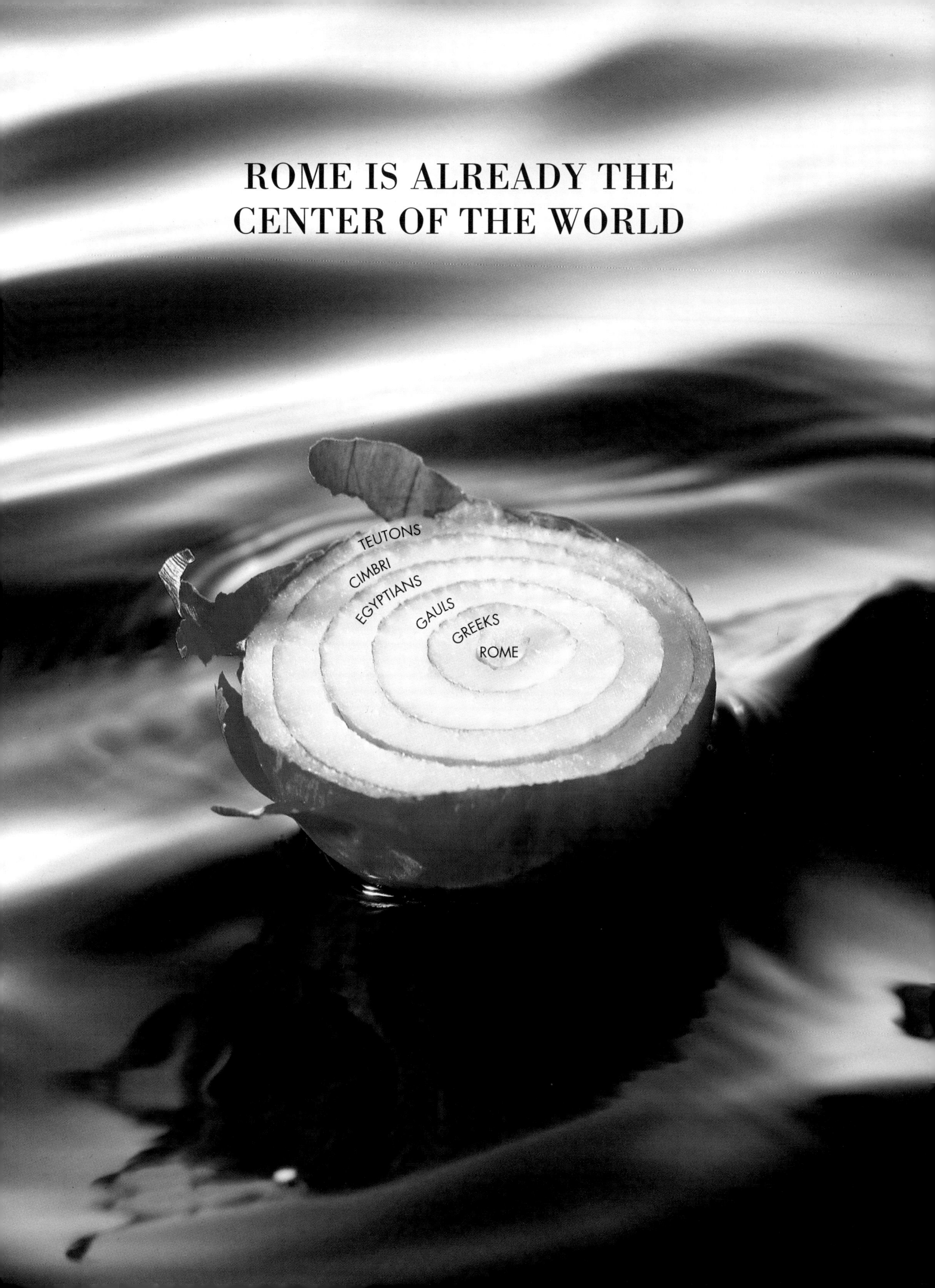
TEUTONS
CIMBRI
EGYPTIANS
GAULS
GREEKS
ROME

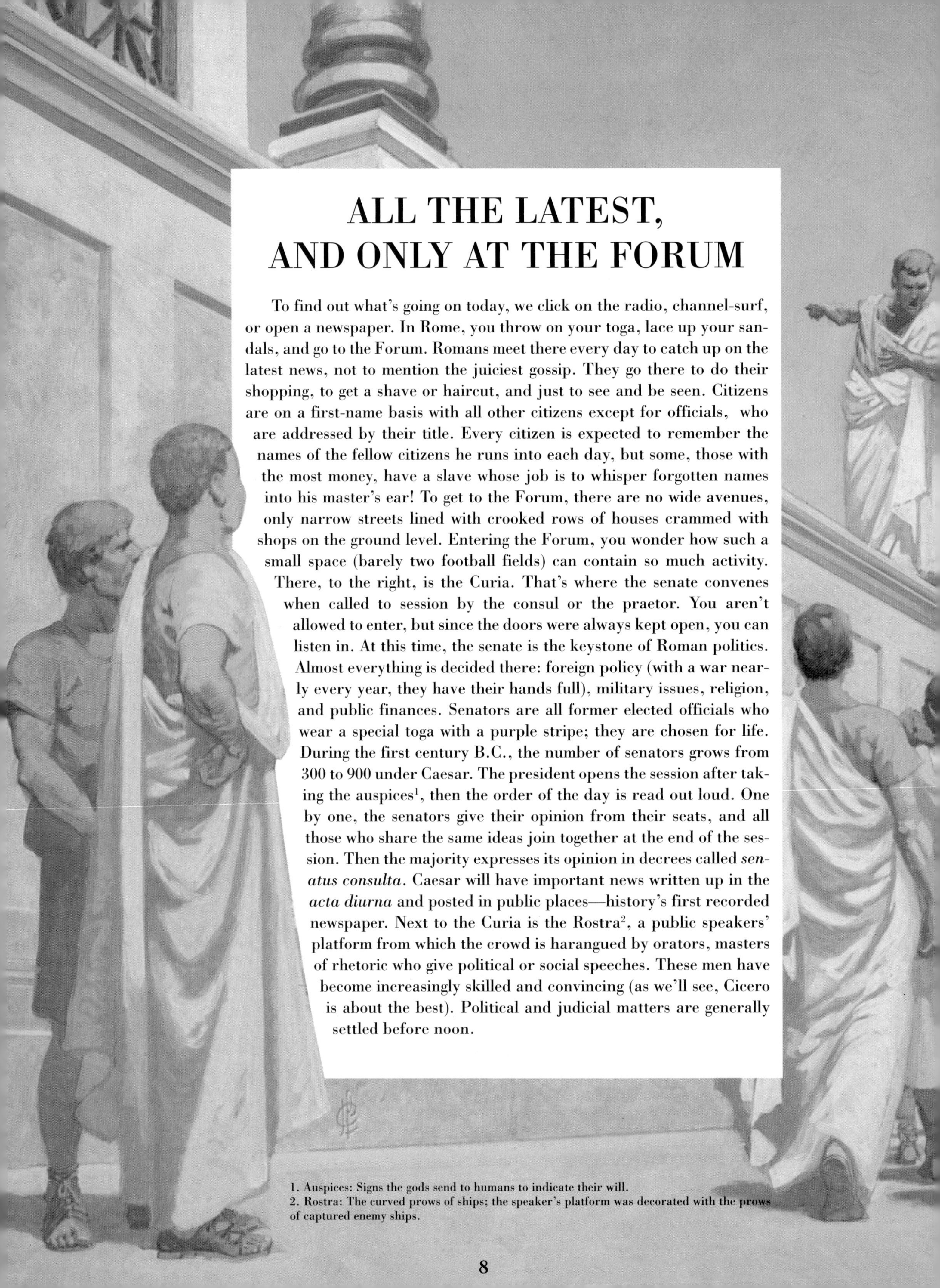

ALL THE LATEST, AND ONLY AT THE FORUM

To find out what's going on today, we click on the radio, channel-surf, or open a newspaper. In Rome, you throw on your toga, lace up your sandals, and go to the Forum. Romans meet there every day to catch up on the latest news, not to mention the juiciest gossip. They go there to do their shopping, to get a shave or haircut, and just to see and be seen. Citizens are on a first-name basis with all other citizens except for officials, who are addressed by their title. Every citizen is expected to remember the names of the fellow citizens he runs into each day, but some, those with the most money, have a slave whose job is to whisper forgotten names into his master's ear! To get to the Forum, there are no wide avenues, only narrow streets lined with crooked rows of houses crammed with shops on the ground level. Entering the Forum, you wonder how such a small space (barely two football fields) can contain so much activity. There, to the right, is the Curia. That's where the senate convenes when called to session by the consul or the praetor. You aren't allowed to enter, but since the doors were always kept open, you can listen in. At this time, the senate is the keystone of Roman politics. Almost everything is decided there: foreign policy (with a war nearly every year, they have their hands full), military issues, religion, and public finances. Senators are all former elected officials who wear a special toga with a purple stripe; they are chosen for life. During the first century B.C., the number of senators grows from 300 to 900 under Caesar. The president opens the session after taking the auspices[1], then the order of the day is read out loud. One by one, the senators give their opinion from their seats, and all those who share the same ideas join together at the end of the session. Then the majority expresses its opinion in decrees called *senatus consulta*. Caesar will have important news written up in the *acta diurna* and posted in public places—history's first recorded newspaper. Next to the Curia is the Rostra[2], a public speakers' platform from which the crowd is harangued by orators, masters of rhetoric who give political or social speeches. These men have become increasingly skilled and convincing (as we'll see, Cicero is about the best). Political and judicial matters are generally settled before noon.

1. Auspices: Signs the gods send to humans to indicate their will.
2. Rostra: The curved prows of ships; the speaker's platform was decorated with the prows of captured enemy ships.

Gods made in Greece: Roman gods are based on Greek gods, with all their attributes and exploits. Only the name changes.

ZEUS

JUPITER
god of the sky

POSEIDON

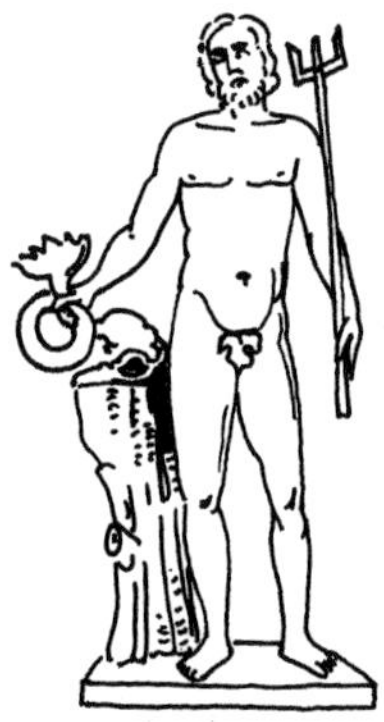

NEPTUNE
god of the sea

ARES

MARS
god of war

HEPHAESTUS

VULCAN
god of fire and metals

HERMES

MERCURY
god of trade and travelers

Romans are more interested in how their chickens eat than in eating them (see the recipe on page 80).

A large part of Roman religion consists of the practice divination[1] and the interpreting of auspices. A few chickens can stop whole armies of strapping soldiers in their tracks just by letting a few grains of chicken feed fall from their beaks. Don't laugh! During the First Punic War (264-241 B.C.), a Roman commander tossed his ship's sacred chickens overboard because they were seasick and wouldn't peck at their food ("If they don't want to eat, let them drink" is what he said). When he lost the battle, his impious gesture was not pardoned by the citizens of Rome.

Religion is everywhere in Rome: temples and statues of the gods abound. The Romans always seem to be appealing to the gods; in fact Polybius, a Greek historian, said, "Romans are more religious than the gods themselves." Before taking any action, whether official or private, auspices are taken; before going to war, the general takes auspices; before opening a session at the senate, auspices are taken. The Romans invoke the names of gods like Hercules and Jupiter, and we still do, by Jove! "It is through religion that we have conquered the universe," said Cicero. Politicians use religion as an instrument of propaganda: the dictator Sulla (138-78 B.C.) gave himself the name Felix, meaning protected by the gods, and Caesar claims to be a descendant of the goddess Venus. All religious acts begin with an animal sacrifice (a ram, pig, or bull). Then a specialist called a *haruspex* examines the entrails for signs from the gods (based on the color, shape, and position of the internal organs). The senate is in charge of Roman religion, but the real head is the chief priest (*Pontifex Maximus*). An official elected for life, he names the *flamens*[2], chooses the Vestal Virgins, and establishes the calendar of observances. This very honorable position is held by Caesar from 63 B.C. until his death.

LET'S TALK . .

In Rome, every official is supposed to observe auspices with the help of a college of advisers called *augurs* (there are 16 under Caesar). They ask Jupiter if he approves of a certain undertaking, such as a general going off to war. Jupiter gives his reply in the form of thunder or lightning or the flights of birds—any natural phenomenon that occurs in his domain, the sky. But even when nothing is asked of Jupiter, he can still send a sign at any time or place, and the augurs have the task of interpreting such messages. What would they make of our weather forecasts!

1. Divination: Interpretation of divine will as expressed in natural phenomena, such as thunder and lightning or the appetite of chickens.

2. Flamen: There were 15 priests, each attached to the cult of a deity. Jupiter's flamen was the supreme priest and had to be present when sacrifices were offered. He wore a vestment, specially woven by his wife, and a bonnet.

Altar frieze of Domitius Ahenobarbarus

DIONYSUS

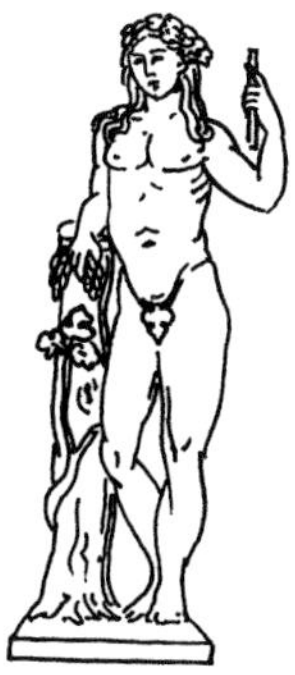

BACCHUS
son of Jupiter, god of wine and fertility

ATHENA

MINERVA
goddess of wisdom

ARTEMIS

DIANA
goddess of the moon and the hunt

DEMETER

CERES
goddess of the harvest

APHRODITE

VENUS
goddess of love and beauty

CHICKEN?

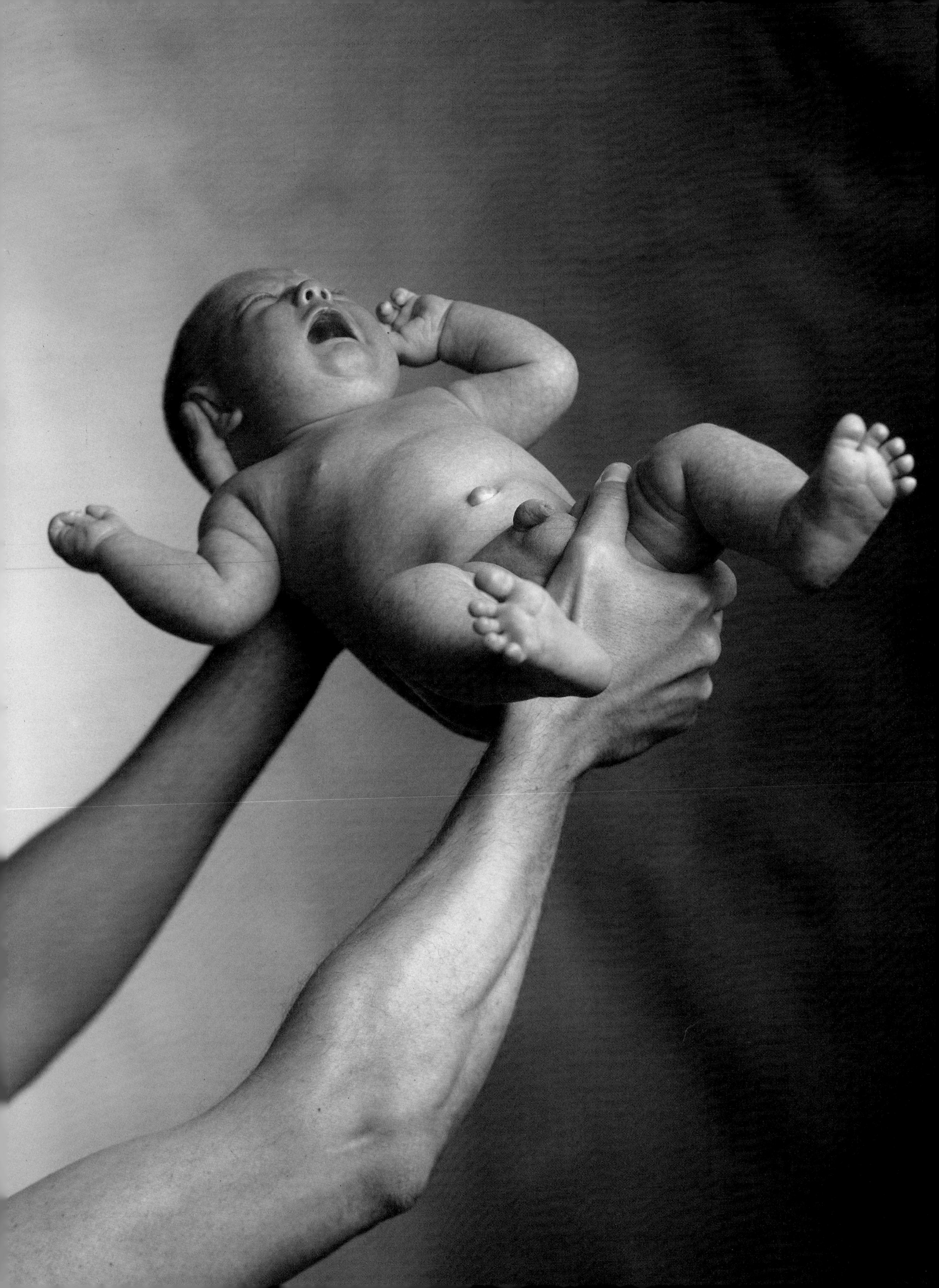

JULIUS MIGHT HAVE BEEN SPURIOUS

Life can be pretty dicey for a Roman baby. The father reigns supreme. He holds the power of life and death over his child. When a baby is born, it is laid on the ground. If the father accepts the child, he picks it up. If he leaves it on the ground, the baby is abandoned or killed; this is most often done because it is deformed or because the family is too poor to keep it. If the child is abandoned, it might be raised by a member of the family or "rescued" by a slave trader. The child then takes the name Spurius, meaning illegitimate. It's tough being a kid.

Luckily for Gaius Julius Caesar, he has two arms, two legs, two ears, and everything else in the right place when his mother gives birth to him on July 13, 101 B.C., in a working-class quarter of Rome called Subura. His father is nice enough to take him in his arms and pick him up. Whew! According to legend Caesar was born by Caesarean section—that's how the operation got its name. But the legend isn't true, as is proved by the simple fact that women who gave birth in that way did not survive, and Caesar's mother died in 58 B.C., when he was a grown man.

A Roman baby

is thought of as modeling clay to be worked into shape. A baby boy is completely wrapped in swaddling clothes for the first few months in order to harden him. In the second month, one arm is released from the swaddling (the right one, so he will be right-handed!). He is bathed daily in cold water, and his nurse massages his face and body. At the age of three, after all these ordeals, the baby is finally fed solid food. A baby is not considered a child (*puer*) until he knows how to walk, talk, and eat. Then boys receive a *bulla*, a gold or leather pendant in the form of a heart or crescent containing good-luck charms. Everything is done to keep the child from getting "soft": no breakfasts in bed, no hot baths. Getting back to little Gaius: after his ninth day in the world, he is finally given his name. Why does he have three names? The newborn is given the first and last names of his father and grandfather: thus Gaius is the *praenomen*, or first name; Julius, the *nomen*, or name of the clan; and Caesar is the *cognomen*, or last name. Born of a noble family that has never really distinguished itself, Caesar belongs on his father's side to the Julian *gens*[1], which claims to be descended from Venus, and on his mother's side to the Aurelian *gens*, a rich plebeian family. His aunt Julia is married to the famous general Marius, glorified for stopping the barbarian invasion. He is head of the *populares* and is up to his seventh consecutive term as consul[2] (a record for the time), while Caesar's father is not even a praetor[3].

AVE
CÆSARE

1. A kind of family clan. Every *gens* has its own clients (like a lord with his vassals in the Middle Ages) who give respect and loyalty to their patron: "The title of patron comes directly after that of father" (Cato). Clients are necessary to the patron. They perform various services and are very useful at election time. In return, the patron gives them money and protection.
2. The highest political office.
3. The office next in rank to consul.

NOT ONLY DO YOU HAVE TO WRITE IN LATIN, YOUHAVETOREADITTOO!

Boys get to go to school, girls have to stay at home. Elementary school begins at age seven, and young Romans go to school from dawn until noon. A *litterator* teaches reading (there are no commas or periods between the words, which are all run together—see the page opposite), writing (on wax tablets with a stylus), and counting (with an abacus). Discipline is harsh. The schoolmaster often uses a *ferula*, a paddle of wood or leather, to rap the knuckles of pupils whose attention wanders. Someone is always "taking the rap" for misbehaving! Parents or slaves take the children to school so they won't run into any unsavory characters along the way.

In Rome, schools are located near the Forum in rooms that are often open to the street, allowing passers-by to drop in and participate. During recess, the children play marbles (made of glass or hazelnuts), catch (with apples), blind man's bluff, and leap-frog. Between the ages of eleven and fifteen, children attend secondary school and are taught grammar by a *grammaticus*. Greek, the second language of the time, is also taught, and the students begin to study the works of Homer, Plato, and Hesiod. Between the ages of sixteen and eighteen, the students are introduced to rhetoric, the art of persuasive speaking and writing. At around sixteen, a boy is no longer considered a child. His parents hold a (toga) party to commemorate the occasion, and the young man exchanges his toga *praetexta*, white with a purple stripe like those of the consuls, for the toga *virilis*, which is entirely white. He is then recognized as a citizen. From that moment on, the young man enters the adult world. He follows his father everywhere, whether to the senate or to a party. In fact, he is not free of parental authority and remains the responsibility of his father until the elder's death. At around eighteen, young nobles journey abroad. This marks the beginning of their working life. As a *contubernalis*, every young noble has to do an "internship" with a general in order to learn about the army and administration.

Caesar as a *contubernalis*: in 81 B.C. Caesar leaves for Asia. He is sent on a mission to Bithynia to "remind" King Nicomedes IV that he has promised boats for a military operation, but the boats haven't arrived. Caesar spends so much time on his mission that people wonder what took him so long. Rumormongers nickname him "the Queen of Bithynia" or "royal whore." Did Caesar really seduce Nicomedes, or has he already become a skillful diplomat? The rumors still fly!

Universities do not yet exist in Rome. Young men who wish to get a "higher education" must cross the Mediterranean to Greece, where they study with the greatest professors of the time. While no longer considered a child, the young man is still not officially an adult. He is considered an adolescent until the age of thirty, so not only is it tough being a kid, it also takes a long time to become an adult.

WEBER

Fragment of Roman tablet

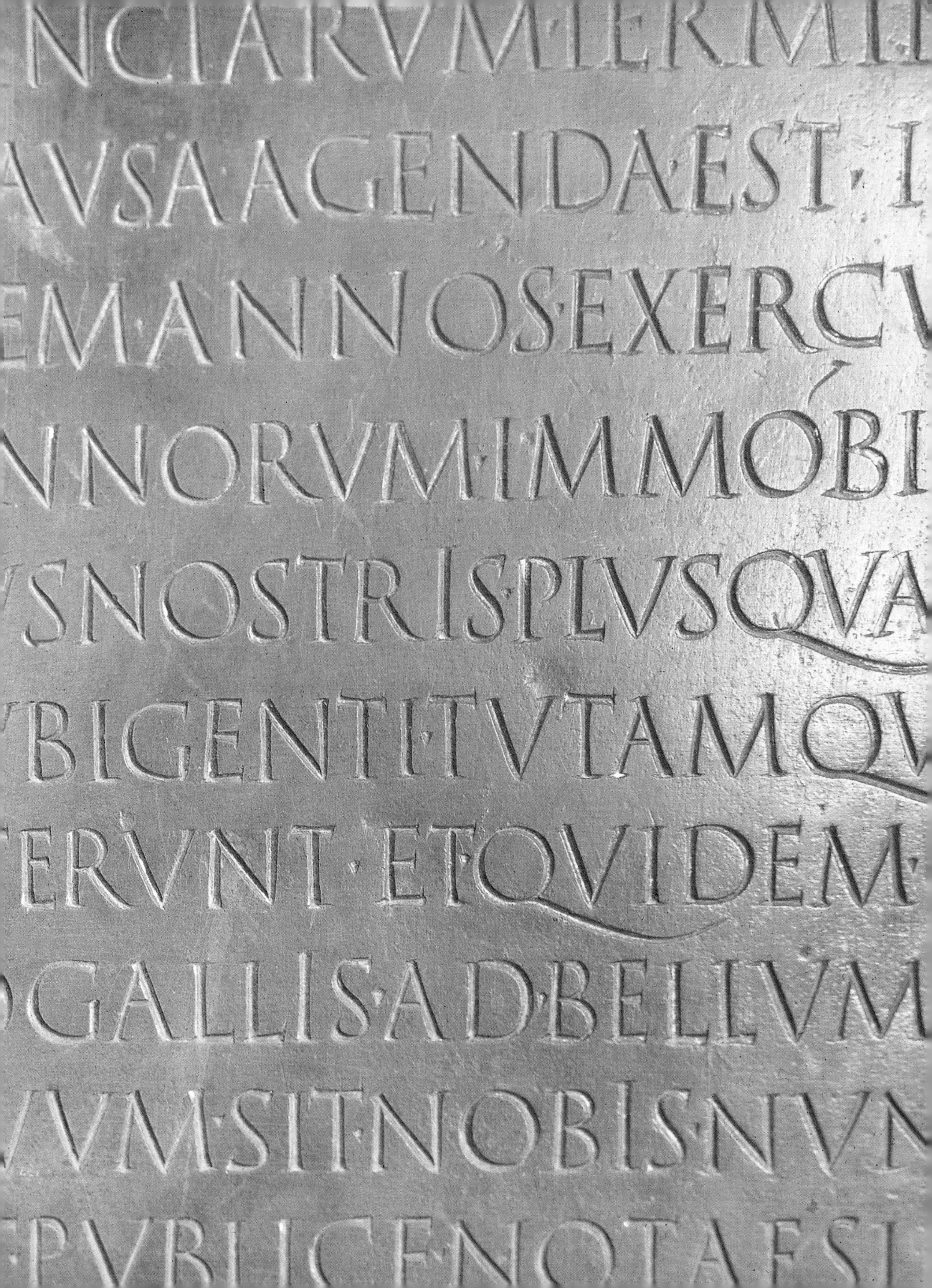
NCIARVM·TERMI
AVSA·AGENDA·EST·I
EMANNOS·EXERCV
NNORVM·IMMOBI
VSNOSTRIS·PLVSQVA
VBIGENTI·TVTAMQV
ERVNT·ET·QVIDEM·
OGALLIS·AD·BELLVM
VVM·SIT·NOBIS·NVN
PVBLICE·NOTA·ESI

LEXICVM

AEDILIS (aedile): Roman public official in charge of public buildings, street maintenance, works, and games.

AGER PUBLICUS: The public land, managed by Roman officials.

AGER ROMANUS: The territory of Rome.

BIENNIUM: The period of two years one must wait between terms of office.

CENSUS: The registration of names and assessment of property every five years.

CENTURIA (century): A military unit of one hundred men.

CIVITAS: Roman citizenship with all rights (*opptimo jure*), or without the right to vote or be elected (*sine suffragio*).

COMITIA: Assembly.

CONSUL: Title of the two chief magistrates and military leaders who serve concurrently for a one-year period.

CURIA: Principal meeting place of the senate.

CURSUS HONORUM: The prescribed career path leading to the office of consul.

DILECTUS: Mustering of troops for a military campaign.

GENS: Clan; for example, the Julian gens, from which Caesar's family descends.

IMPERIUM: Military power given to consuls and praetors.

INTERCESSIO: The right of a plebeian tribune to oppose any measure that is contrary to the interests of the people.

JUSTITIUM: Suspension of public activity in Rome on unfavorable days.

Legio (legion): A military corps of about 4,200 men.

Lictor: A guard who precedes Roman officials bearing an ax surrounded by a bundle of sticks. The more important the official, the greater the number of lictors.

Obnuntiatio: The announcement of bad omens.

Optimates: The conservative politicians in the senate.

Pomerium: The sacred boundary of Rome, which no one could cross bearing arms.

Pontifex Maximus: The high priest of Roman religion, elected for life.

Populares: The politicians supporting the people.

Praetor: Roman magistrate who takes care of judicial matters and stands in for the consul.

Provocatio ad populum: The right of any citizen condemned by an official to appeal before an assembly.

Quaestor: The elected official in charge of finances.

Res publica: A public matter.

Rogatio: A bill or proposed law.

Senatus: The senate, or council of elders. It handles foreign policy, war, and religion.

Senatus consultum: The report of the senate's proceedings giving the opinion of the majority.

Sestertius (sesterce): Roman coin. 1 sesterce = 1/4 denarius = (very roughly) 63 cents.

Suffragium: Oral vote.

Tabella: Secret ballot introduced in 140 B.C.

Tribuni plebis (tribunes of the plebs): Officials representing the people who have the right of *intercessio* (see above) and are sacrosanct, meaning protected by religious sanction against assault.

Triumphus (triumph): Celebration in Rome in honor of a great victory.

STUDENT CHOSEN MOST LIKELY TO SUCCEED, GAIUS JULIUS CAESAR

FIRST PRIZE IN LATIN

Caesar masters his native language magnificently and will later use it to turn tricky situations to his advantage.

FIRST PRIZE IN GREEK

Caesar is totally bilingual; the last words he will speak are in Greek: "You, too, my child," spoken to Brutus, whom Caesar thinks of as a son, but who is one of his murderers!

FIRST PRIZE IN RIDING

Caesar is very athletic and will spend a large part of his military life on horseback.

FIRST PRIZE IN PUBLIC SPEAKING

His grammaticus *Marcus Antonius Gnipho teaches Caesar to express himself well. According to Cicero, who certainly knew what he was talking about, one simply has to* "docere, delectare, movere"*: to teach, please, and move.*

FIRST PRIZE IN HISTORY

Caesar's education covers many subjects, and he becomes very learned. He is fascinated by Alexander the Great. In Cadiz, he will lament before a statue of Alexander, who died three centuries earlier, that at the age of thirty Alexander had already conquered the world (the Mediterranean world, that is) while he himself hasn't even won a major battle!

FIRST PRIZE FOR DARING

Around 78 B.C., he is on his way to Rhodes to study with the great master Apollonius Molo when he is kidnapped by pirates who demand a ransom (which Caesar thinks too small!). Once the ransom is paid, Caesar is freed after forty days of captivity. Then he returns to the pirates, takes back his money, and has his former abductors crucified. Talk about revenge!

FIRST PRIZE IN SPORTS

Every good Roman is expected to be athletic. Caesar is exceptionally sturdy despite his slight build. He moves fast—he often arrives at his destination before the messengers he has sent ahead to announce his approach.

FIRST PRIZE IN PHILOSOPHY

His structured thoughts and well-chosen arguments succeed in winning over more than one person—and more than one angry crowd.

FIRST PRIZE IN GRAMMAR

It is Gnipho again who teaches Caesar syntax. He will use his knowledge later in life when writing his Gallic War *and* Civil War.

FIRST PRIZE IN SWIMMING

Caesar swims like a fish. This is what will save him during the battle of Alexandria, when he is forced to dive into the water.

IN ROME, IT'S MORE IMPORTANT TO LOOK

A Roman is nothing without the regard of others. He needs to be seen and heard to exist socially. Roman citizenship is passed down from father to son, and each citizen has the right to vote and to be elected, to get married, to own land, to participate in the priesthood, to appeal to the people in criminal trials, and to sue. He has to participate in the census (the registration of citizens and their property according to the five classes of wealth[1]) every five years and serve as a soldier (between the ages of seventeen and forty-six) when Rome needs him. Luckily, he pays no taxes, which is not the case for noncitizens. Despite Socrates' 300-year-old words, "Know thyself," the motto at the time seems to be "Know thyself through the eyes of others." Since a Roman spends most of his day away from home, his smallest action is subject to criticism or praise. There are always witnesses hanging around in the streets, and every gesture is interpreted, every word repeated, every act praised or disparaged. Romans don't like being alone. They need to feel recognized. The magistrate is preceded by his lictors (who act as bodyguards in case of a disturbance). The wealthy Roman is followed by his clients and slaves.

1. 1st class: fortune estimated at 250,000 sesterces (1 sesterce = about 63 cents), or $157,000, 2nd class: 75,000 sesterces, or $47,250, 3rd class: 25,000 sesterces,

MARVELOUS THAN TO FEEL MARVELOUS

r $15,750, 4th class: 12,500 sesterces, or $7,875, 5th class: 1,000 sesterces, or $630.

THE GAME OF ROMAN PO

In Rome, just wanting to be a politician doesn't mean you can become one. To be a government official, Condition 1: you have to be a Roman citizen (have a Roman father). Condition 2: you need lots of money because you have to pay a bunch of hangers-on called clients. But the more clients you have, the more votes you can count on. You have to know what the three pillars of politics are: magistrates (politicians), the senate, and the *comitia* (people's assemblies). You are not allowed to be the only one elected to an office (unless you happen to be dictator), so there are always at least two officials per post.

You need patience, and you must avoid pitfalls.

You can begin your political career only after ten years of military service (minimum age: 27).

Once elected to a post, you can hold it for only one year.

Between your first post and that of consul, you are asked to wait about ten years.

You can run for another term of consul only every ten years. Good news: there are many opportunities to be elected because there are lots of posts to fill (and also a lot of money to hand out).

The best way to go is the *cursus honorum*, or honorable career path. It is a tricky route, but Caesar comes through it with flying colors.

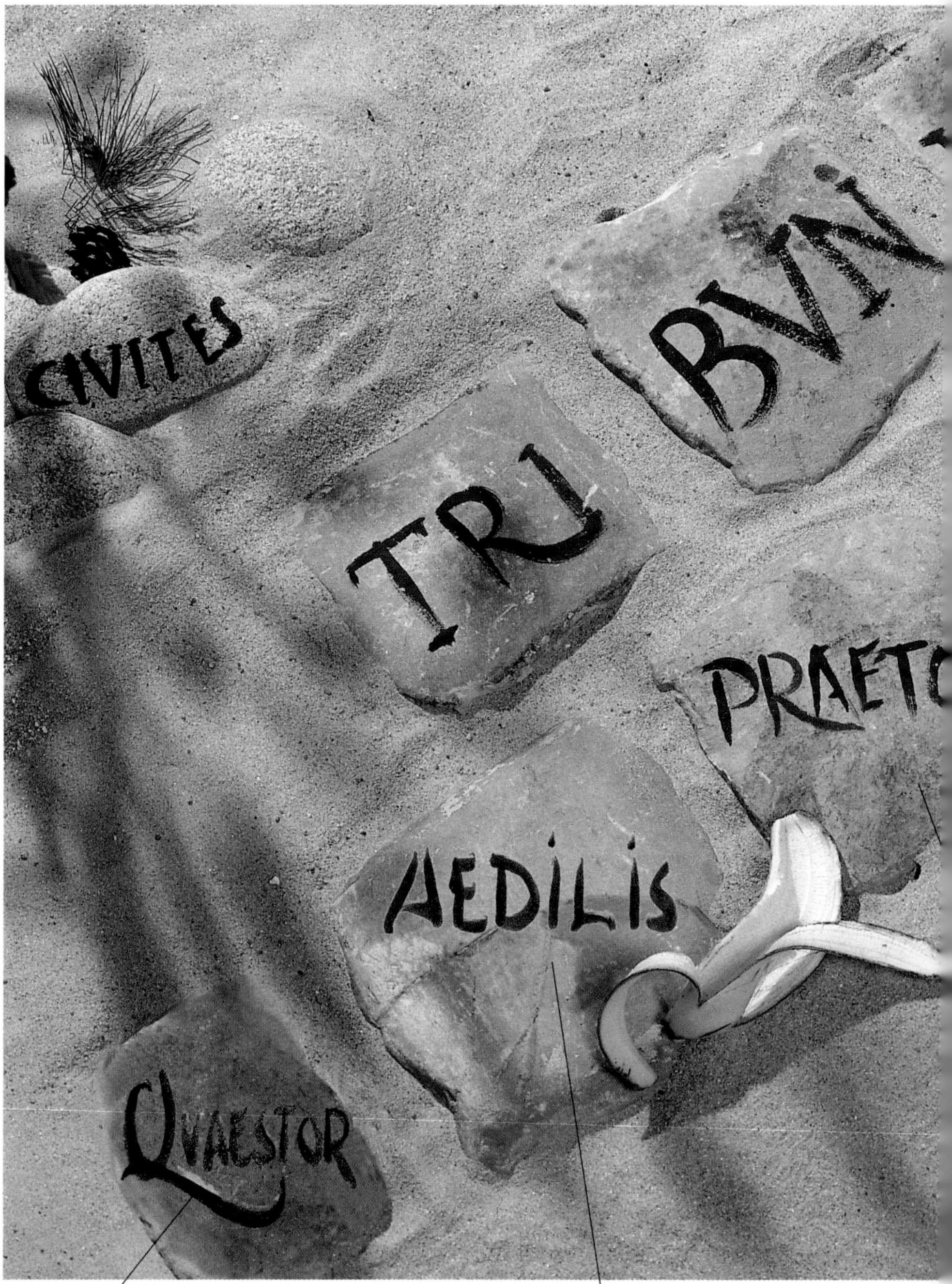
CIVITES
TRI
BVN
PRAET
AEDILIS
QVAESTOR

Quaestor is the first office you must get elected to. You'll need to be 30. This post puts you in charge of government funds. You can hold this office in Rome or in a province (under Caesar there are 40 quaestors because of all the lands he conquered).

At age 37, you can become aedile, in charge of the upkeep of monuments and streets, public works, and stocking the markets, not to mention sponsoring public amusements: that's where the people are really watching you. You're supposed to go all out to make sure the people have fun—and with your own money, too!

TICS IS FULL OF PITFALLS

If you happen to be a plebeian, or commoner, you can become tribune of the plebeians. As such, you'll look after the interests of the common people. As tribune, you'll have the right of *intercessio*, which means you can intervene if a measure goes against the wishes of the plebs, as the plebeians are called. You also have the right to convene the senate and the right to veto a measure. You are untouchable because the rights of the people are inviolable.

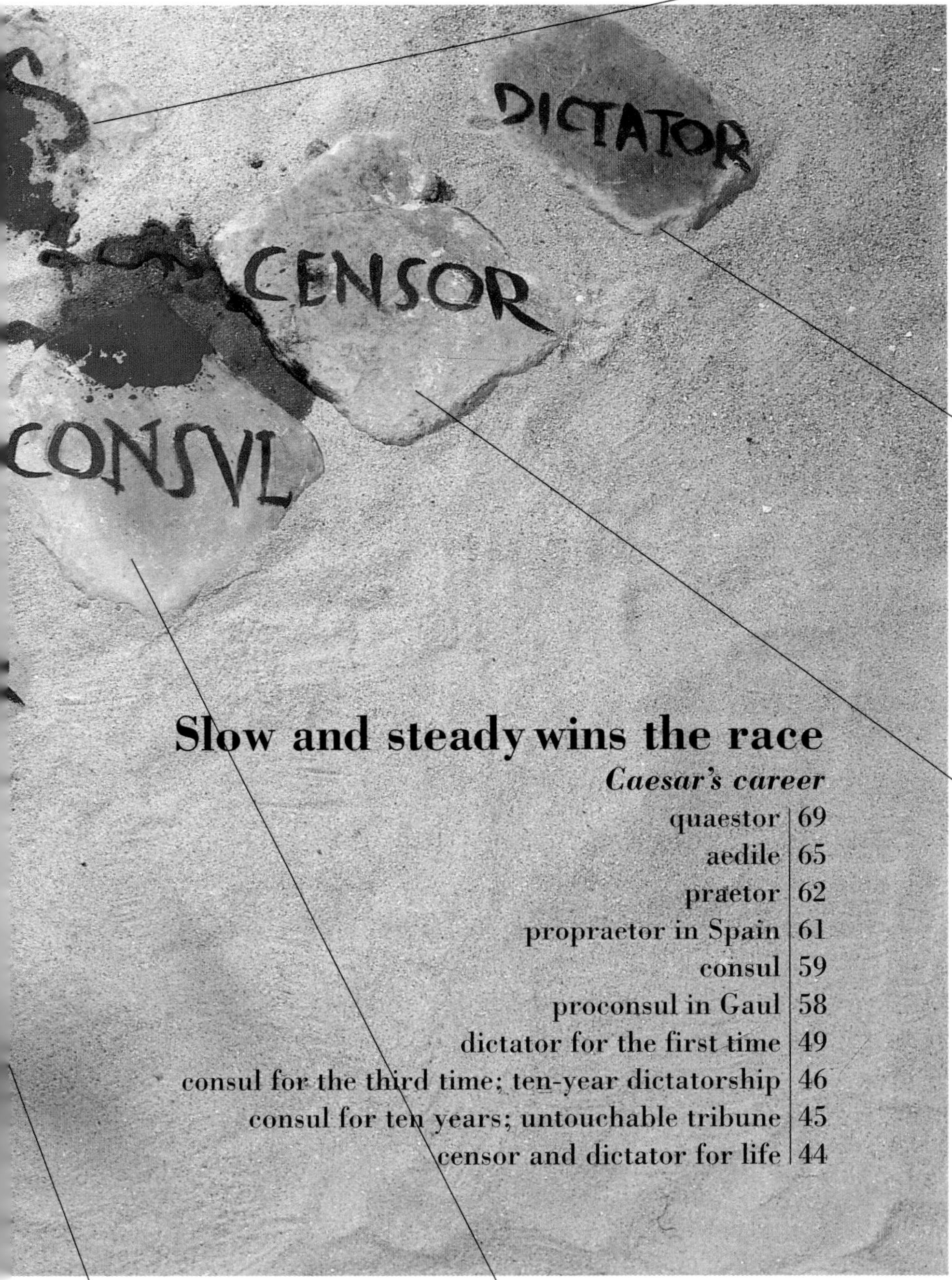
DICTATOR
CENSOR
CONSVL

Slow and steady wins the race

Caesar's career

quaestor	69
aedile	65
praetor	62
propraetor in Spain	61
consul	59
proconsul in Gaul	58
dictator for the first time	49
consul for the third time; ten-year dictatorship	46
consul for ten years; untouchable tribune	45
censor and dictator for life	44

In an emergency, you can be named dictator by the senate for a six-month period only, because as dictator you have unlimited power.

When you get older, you can become a censor, but you need to have been a consul first. As censor, it is your job to draw up the list of Roman citizens and to recruit senators. Censors cannot be reelected.

Next, you can become praetor: they administer justice and fill in for the consuls when they are called away from Rome. After holding this position, you are sent to a province to be propraetor for one year.

Now you're 41, ready to become consul. As consul, you have executive power as well as being *imperium militae* ("commander in chief"), with powers to raise an army and command military expeditions anywhere up to the *pomerium*, Rome's sacred city limits. You are an eponymous consul, meaning that you lend your name to the year in which you hold office. After your term, you are named proconsul in a province for one year.

BE CAREFUL! HIDING BEHIND

In Rome of the sixties (B.C., that is) the ball of power is in the air, and a handful of players is fighting one another to grab it. Presented in decreasing order of importance, here are those men, with explanations of why they're having such a hard time staying friends with Caesar:

POMPEY
(106-48 B.C.)

*Great Roman general, victorious over King Mithradates of Pontus in 64 B.C. and married to Caesar's daughter, Julia (Pompey is 47 and she's 17!). He is used to finishing what others begin and taking all the credit for it. Pompey is Caesar's ally, along with Crassus, when the three form the First Triumvirate (*trium *for "three," and* viri *for "men") in 60 B.C. The Roman historian Suetonius wrote that the three men swore "to oppose all legislation of which any one of them might disapprove." Democracy is clearly running out of steam. So how did these three men ever get together in the first place? French historian Jérôme Carcopino had the answer: "Crassus had the money, Pompey his troops and conquests, and Caesar, genius, divine glory, and the adoration of the crowds." Because the alliance is antidemocratic, it is completely illegal. But it is formed to ensure that Caesar is elected consul the following year. And it works. Ties between Pompey and Caesar become frayed, however, after the death of Julia in September 54 B.C. By the time civil war (49-45 B.C.) breaks out, the two men hate each other. After his defeat at Pharsalus against Caesar's armies, Pompey is assassinated on the Egyptian coast in 48 B.C. on the orders of the Egyptian king, who sides with Caesar. Pompey's sons continue his fight until the defeat at Munda (Spain) in March 45 B.C. The victory does not come easily. Here are Caesar's own words on the subject: "Everywhere I have fought for victory, but at Munda I fought to save my life."*

CRASSUS
(115-53 B.C.)

Certainly the richest man in Rome, Crassus is Caesar's principal financial backer and one of the First Triumvirate. Named proconsul in Syria in 55 B.C., Crassus is killed during a battle against the Parthians in June 53 B.C. His death brings the First Triumvirate to its official end, but for the two remaining men, the breakup occurred long before.

CICERO
(106-43 B.C.)

Cicero is described by Appian (a Roman historian of the first century A.D.) as a "very popular orator and lawyer." As consul in 63 B.C. he exposes Catiline's conspiracy. Exiled by Caesar in 58 B.C., he changes his tune and declares himself on Caesar's side, which gives him the opportunity to return to Rome a year later. After Caesar's death, he sides with Octavian, Caesar's adopted son, against Mark Antony, whom he denounces in fiery speeches called Philippics. In revenge, Mark Antony has Cicero's throat cut. Ouch.

EVERY FRIEND COULD BE A FOE

Catiline
(108-62 B.C.)
Catiline is a ruined noble who wants to be consul; his proposals include a general cancellation of debts and land distribution. When he is defeated, he decides to use violent means to overthrow the Roman state. The facts of the conspiracy are leaked to Cicero by Catiline's loose-lipped mistress. His followers, known as Catilinarians, are arrested, condemned without appeal, and strangled in prison. Catiline himself flees and is killed in battle. The affair does little credit to anyone except, perhaps, Caesar, who makes a daring plea on behalf of the conspirators.

Mark Antony
(83-30 B.C.)
Mark Antony is Caesar's first lieutenant. He becomes his cavalry master, that is, his second-in-command. Upon the death of Caesar, he sets off in search of the murderers while Octavian is away, but then the two become rivals, and Antony is crushed at Actium in 31 B.C. He and his mistress, Cleopatra, commit suicide.

WEBER

Clodius
(93-52 B.C.)
Claudius creates a scandal when he disguises himself as a woman to enter Caesar's house during the Bona Dea festival; Cicero tries to prosecute him for sacrilege, but Claudius bribes his way free. Then Claudius decides to run for tribune of the plebs. But there's a catch: only a plebeian can hold that office. With Caesar's help, Claudius gets himself adopted by a plebeian and changes his name to Clodius, which sounds less upper-crust. Once elected, he takes revenge on Cicero, passing two laws directly targeting Cicero, who was responsible for the execution, without right to appeal, of the Catilinarians. Cicero goes into self-imposed exile. Two armed gangs form, one supporters of Clodius, Caesars's protege, and the other of Milo, who is secretly backed by Pompey; and bloody rioting reigns in the streets of Rome until Clodius is wounded during street fighting and, on Milo's orders, is finished off in an inn.

Brutus
(85-42 B.C.)
Brutus is the nephew of Cato of Utica and the son of Servilia, Caesar's mistress. Caesar saves Brutus's life after the defeat at Pharsalus (48 B.C.) and names him propraetor in Cisalpine Gaul. Not one to show much gratitude, it is Brutus who hatches the plot to rid Rome of the man who would be king—Caesar. With his conspirators, he assassinates Caesar on March 15, 44 B.C., then flees, gathers troops, and is beaten at Philippi (Macedonia) in 42 B.C. by Mark Antony and Octavian, Caesar's successors. He takes his own life.

Octavian
(63 B.C.- A.D. 14)
Octavian is the grand-nephew of Caesar, who adopts him and makes him his heir (Caesar has no sons of his own). After ridding himself of Mark Antony at Actium, Octavian makes Egypt a Roman province, receives the honorary title Augustus (a title that will be used by all Roman emperors), and becomes the first Roman emperor in 27 B.C. under the name Augustus.

"ROMANS, LOCK YOUR WIVES AWAY! HERE COMES THE BALD SEDUCER!"

He's no sex symbol, but Caesar has sex appeal. His soldiers call him "the bald seducer"—the hairless hunk, if you will. He has charisma and a way with words, too. As a young man, he shocks Rome by letting the folds of his toga drag along the ground—is he just a slob, or does he do it on purpose? Unhappy about his premature baldness, Caesar wears a crown of laurel leaves whenever he can get away with it and combs his few remaining strands of hair forward. Caesar's hair inspires Cicero, one of his biggest enemies, to remark, "When I see his hair so carefully arranged, and observe him adjusting it with one finger, I cannot imagine it should enter into such a man's thoughts to subvert the Roman state."

He's in the habit of choosing his mistresses from among the wives of his friends or even his enemies. Maybe he wants to live up to the reputation of his ancestor Venus!

He's said to have had an affair with the king of Bithynia, with whom he spent so much time closing a deal for boats that everyone thought they must have worked it out in private. This adventure earns him the title "Queen of Bithynia" or even "Caesar, every woman's man and every man's woman." Caesar has a reputation of being a sex fiend, but he seems no worse than other Romans in that respect, and at least he doesn't drink—which inspires Marcus Cato to call Caesar "the only sober man who ever tried to wreck the Constitution."

Caesar's married life, like that of any self-respecting noble, is rather turbulent. At 16, he marries Cornelia, daughter of Sulla, who is dictator and Caesar's political adversary. At 17 he becomes the father of Julia, his only child. At 33, he marries Pompeia, Sulla's granddaughter. By the time he divorces her following the Bona Dea scandal (see Marriage, Roman Style), he's already having an affair with Servilia, mother of Brutus, one of his future assassins.

At 41, he marries Calpurnia, his last wife.

WANT TO MAKE YOURSELF SEDUCTIVE TO CAESAR? FOLLOW OUR BEAUTY TIPS!

This year, dark hair is in. Blondes have two options: dye your hair with soap from Gaul—a blend of beechwood ashes and goat fat—or buy yourself a wig at the Forum. Hair styling hasn't been the same since the curling iron came out: curls on curls are all the rage.

For skin that's soft and radiant, try the newest cream from Circe Plus: it has bread mixed with barley flour, dried eggs, narcissus bulbs, and stag horn.

For sparkling teeth, use a pumice stone. Should you happen to lose a tooth, replace it with a gold one held in place by a thread.

Apply liniment to your face—this super foundation is handmade from crocodile excrement. Remember: pale face tints are in this year.

For your eyes, a bit of ash will do the trick, and a hint of saltpeter highlights the cheeks.

Caesar's favorite perfume is fleur de vigne, *"flower of the vine." The most sought-after scent is cinnamon, but it costs ten times as much (300* denarii*) as any other perfume.*

Don't wear all your fibulae *(brooches) on the same day. Be discreet: a nice pair of gold earrings and a pearl pendant are plenty this century.*

Small bosoms are solidly in. Those overly well-endowed use leather bands to hold in their bust. When you go out, show off your best features and hide the rest. Pretty hands? Use them to express yourself when you speak! Dingy teeth? Try not to smile, and whatever you do, don't laugh!

CICERO THRILLS THEM IN THE GALLERY

Cicero is born in Arpinum, 60 miles southeast of Rome, in 106 B.C. He is a "new man," meaning he is the first in his family to go into politics. Elected consul in 63 B.C., he is better known for his talent as an excellent

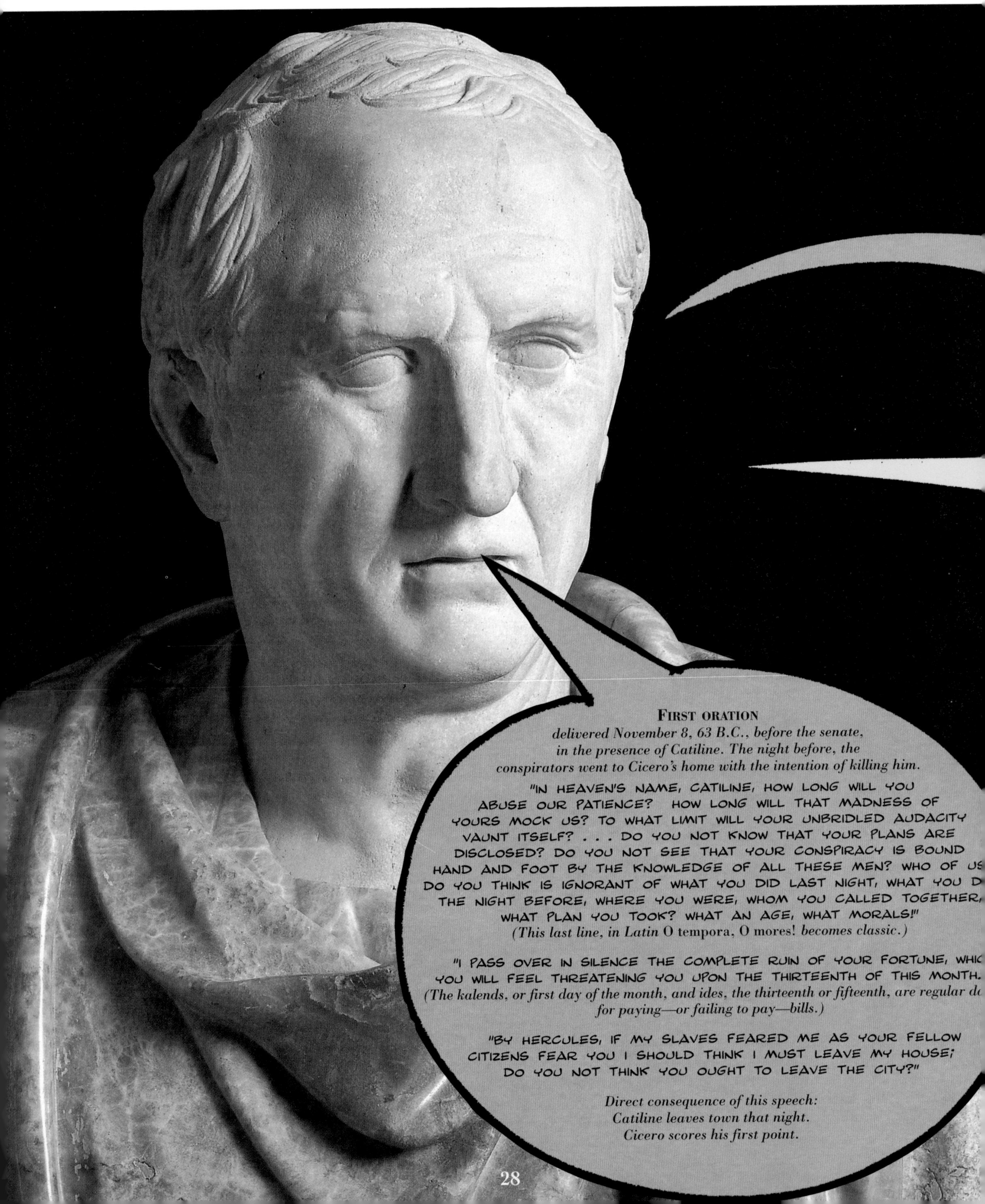
FIRST ORATION
delivered November 8, 63 B.C., before the senate, in the presence of Catiline. The night before, the conspirators went to Cicero's home with the intention of killing him.
"IN HEAVEN'S NAME, CATILINE, HOW LONG WILL YOU ABUSE OUR PATIENCE? HOW LONG WILL THAT MADNESS OF YOURS MOCK US? TO WHAT LIMIT WILL YOUR UNBRIDLED AUDACITY VAUNT ITSELF? . . . DO YOU NOT KNOW THAT YOUR PLANS ARE DISCLOSED? DO YOU NOT SEE THAT YOUR CONSPIRACY IS BOUND HAND AND FOOT BY THE KNOWLEDGE OF ALL THESE MEN? WHO OF US DO YOU THINK IS IGNORANT OF WHAT YOU DID LAST NIGHT, WHAT YOU D THE NIGHT BEFORE, WHERE YOU WERE, WHOM YOU CALLED TOGETHER, WHAT PLAN YOU TOOK? WHAT AN AGE, WHAT MORALS!"
(This last line, in Latin O tempora, O mores! becomes classic.)
"I PASS OVER IN SILENCE THE COMPLETE RUIN OF YOUR FORTUNE, WHIC YOU WILL FEEL THREATENING YOU UPON THE THIRTEENTH OF THIS MONTH.
(The kalends, or first day of the month, and ides, the thirteenth or fifteenth, are regular d for paying—or failing to pay—bills.)
"BY HERCULES, IF MY SLAVES FEARED ME AS YOUR FELLOW CITIZENS FEAR YOU I SHOULD THINK I MUST LEAVE MY HOUSE; DO YOU NOT THINK YOU OUGHT TO LEAVE THE CITY?"
Direct consequence of this speech: Catiline leaves town that night. Cicero scores his first point.

orator, possibly unequaled in all the history of Rome, than for his political skill. His *Orations against Catiline*, a series of four famous speeches, constitute one of the masterpieces of Latin literature. Let's review the facts: in 63 B.C., Cicero is consul and denounces the conspiracy of Catiline, a bankrupt noble who wants to kill Cicero and set fire to twelve districts of Rome.

SECOND ORATION

delivered the following day at the Forum.

"THE CITY REJOICES BECAUSE IT HAS SPEWED OUT THAT PESTILENCE AND CAST IT FORTH. I WAS EVEN SORRY BECAUSE TOO FEW WENT WITH HIM WHEN HE WENT AWAY. WOULD THAT HE HAD TAKEN WITH HIM ALL HIS FORCES! . . . LET THEM GO OUT, LET THEM DEPART . . . I WILL SHOW THE WAY: HE WENT BY THE AURELIAN ROAD; IF THEY CHOOSE TO HURRY THEY WILL OVERTAKE HIM BY EVENING."

(A touch of humor is always appreciated.)

"WHAT POISONER IN ALL ITALY, WHAT GLADIATOR, WHAT ROBBER, WHAT ASSASSIN, WHAT PARRICIDE, WHAT FORGER OF WILLS, WHAT CHEAT, WHAT GLUTTON, WHAT SPENDTHRIFT, WHAT ADULTERER, WHAT INFAMOUS WOMAN, WHAT CORRUPTER OF YOUTH, WHAT PROFLIGATE, WHAT ABANDONED CHARACTER CAN BE FOUND WHO DOES NOT ADMIT THAT HE HAS LIVED ON MOST INTIMATE TERMS WITH CATILINE? WHAT MURDER HAS BEEN COMMITTED THROUGH ALL THESE YEARS WITHOUT HIM?

(Cicero is known for his tendency to exaggerate.)

Direct consequence of this speech: the Catilinarians are arrested that same evening. Cicero scores his second point.

THIRD ORATION

delivered on December 3 at the Forum before the people.

"SINCE I HAVE DISCLOSED, MADE CLEAR, AND FULLY RECOUNTED THESE EVENTS IN THE SENATE, I WILL NOW BRIEFLY LAY ALL BEFORE YOU, CITIZENS."

(Here we discover what a modest guy Cicero is.)

"IN RETURN FOR THESE GREAT SERVICES, CITIZENS, I ASK FROM YOU NO REWARD FOR COURAGE, NO INSIGNIA OF HONOR, NO MONUMENT OF PRAISE, EXCEPT THE ETERNAL MEMORY OF THIS DAY."

(Thank goodness his modesty doesn't keep him from speaking up.)

Direct consequence of this speech: Cicero receives from the people, for the first time in Rome, the title of Pater Patriae, *"father of his country." The second one to receive the title will be Caesar. Cicero scores his third point.*

FOURTH ORATION

delivered on December 5 to the senate. Cicero now speaks on the fate of the Catilinarians: death or life in prison? Cicero opts for the former.

"I SEE, CONSCRIPT FATHERS *[the senators]*, THE COUNTENANCES AND EYES OF ALL YOU TURNED TOWARD ME. I SEE THAT YOU ARE ANXIOUS, NOT ONLY ABOUT YOUR OWN DANGER AND THAT OF THE STATE, BUT ALSO, IF THAT IS AVERTED, ABOUT MY DANGER." *(He reminds them of the attempt on his life, as well as his courage.)*

"BUT, IF THE POWER OF CRIMINALS SHALL DISAPPOINT MY EXPECTATION AND SHALL TRIUMPH, I COMMEND TO YOU MY LITTLE SON . . . IF YOU WILL BUT REMEMBER THAT HE IS THE SON OF THE MAN WHO SAVED THE ENTIRE STATE, RISKING HIMSELF ALONE."

(He tries to move his audience, which is the secret for success of any speech.)

Direct consequence: the Catilinarians are strangled in prison that very evening. Fourth point for Cicero. Catiline is killed on January 5, 62 B.C., during a battle. Cicero is exiled in 58 B.C. for giving the order to execute the Catilinarians without an appeal.

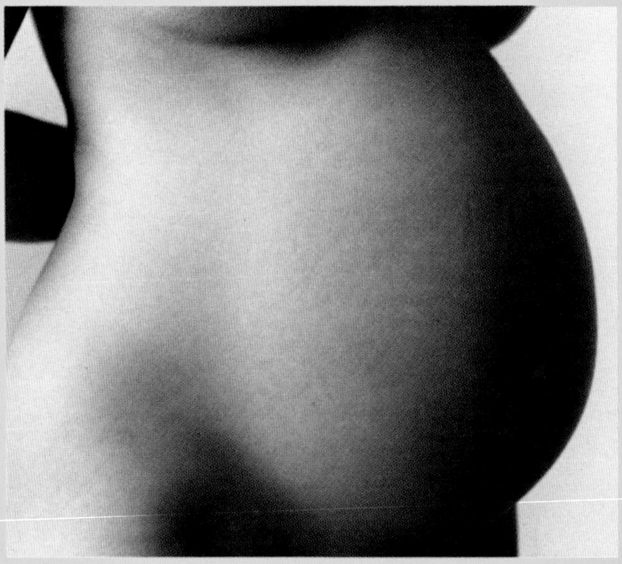

MARRIAGE, ROMAN STYLE: THE WOMAN IS FIRST AND FOREMOST A WOMB

When you are noble and influential in Rome, getting married is really a family affair; you marry into another noble and influential family. The parents make the arrangements without consulting the future couple. When a woman marries, she passes from her father's authority to her husband's. Her role is to have babies and to take care of the house. Women are first and foremost wombs.

Nevertheless, at the end of the republic, the status of married women changes. They become more independent, both financially and personally.

During this period, marriages, remarriages, and divorces are frequent, especially in a society where alliances and friendships are generally of short duration. Pondering this, Cato wrote, "It is intolerable that the public authority is prostituted through marriages and that women are used by cronies to distribute provinces, armies, and power among themselves." Pompey and Caesar each have had several wives: Pompey marries Caesar's daughter, Julia. When she dies, Caesar wants to marry Pompey's daughter and give Pompey his grand-niece, but Pompey refuses this offer, instead marrying the widow of Crassus, who was the third member of the First Triumvirate.

One might well ask if marital fidelity exists, since Rome seems to be a hub of degeneracy. The answer is not really, at least not among the elite. In public, Romans are modest; kissing is a no-no outdoors. But at home, the head of the household makes up for it with his slaves, male or female. Spouses are often indifferent toward each other. Each leads his or her own life but must be careful not to let any scandal erupt. In Rome, everyone makes fun of Pompey's love life: every time he meets a new love goddess, he says it's the real thing finally and forever and talks about it in public like a teenager in love for the first time.

Is Rome really so immoral? Perhaps not: many later historians made Rome sound far more wicked than it may actually have been. Then again, there's always that bit of graffiti found on a wall in Caesar's city: "Baths, wine, and sex ruin our bodies. But what makes life worth living except baths, wine, and sex?"

The bona dea scandal
Clodius, a young patrician, is infatuated with Pompeia, Caesar's wife. He decides to visit her on the evening of the celebration of the cult of Bona Dea, when all men are banished from the house; even statues of men are covered up with sheets. To get around this, Clodius disguises himself as a female harpist. His voice gives him away, however, and a scandal erupts. Caesar divorces Pompeia but refuses to speak against her in court because, he says, "Caesar's wife should be above suspicion." As for Clodius, he is pardoned.

A marriage made in Rome
On the day of the wedding, the bride puts on a white tunic and does her hair in six braids held in place by a band. She wears an orange veil. In the morning, the guests meet in front of the bridegroom's house and offer a sacrifice. Then the wedding is performed in front of ten witnesses, who sign their names on the contract. A woman at the head of the procession joins the hands of the bride and groom. A benediction is requested and the couple offers another sacrifice. In the evening, the bride leaves her father's house for her husband's. There, she is carried over the threshold by young men of the wedding party (to keep her from stumbling, which would be taken as a bad omen). She then must recite the following words: Ubi tu Gaius, ego Gaia *("Where you will be Gaius, I will be Gaia").*

CAESAR AND BIBULUS ARE ELECTED

CONSULS! WHO THE HECK IS BIBULUS?

In 59 B.C., Caesar is elected to the office of consul along with Bibulus (remember, two men are elected to each office). The Triumvirate is working. At last Caesar will be able to sit on the curule chair, which is reserved for consuls in the senate. What are his political views? Those of a leader of the *populares*. He opts for policies that are favorable to the people, which goes against the ambitions of the *optimates*, the conservative politicians. Caesar revives the old custom of having whichever of the two consuls is actively serving (they alternate every month) escorted by twelve lictors. The country is being run by the Triumvirate, something that has never happened before in Roman politics. Caesar wants to halt corruption (with which he is familiar, having long practiced it himself) by limiting gifts of money to provincial governors to 10,000 sesterces (*Lex Iulia de pecuniis repetundis*). He makes the proceedings of senate sessions public (*acta Senatus*), as well as political affairs and other news (*acta diurna*). In between laws, he does a little public relations by marrying his daughter off to Pompey and getting married himself to Calpurnia. He ratifies Pompey's actions in Asia (he has given lots of money to kings and princes) against the senate's will, a senate which Caesar purposefully forgets to convene on a regular basis. He makes friends with the equites[1] by offering them a 30 percent reduction on the money that they, being the principal tax collectors (*publicani*) in the provinces, must turn over to the state. He votes in two agrarian laws. The first offers 20,000 Roman citizens, all fathers of three children, land taken from the *ager publicus*, the public land, which is managed by magistrates. The second offers land in Campagna, fertile territory around Rome that is prized by senators. This only increases the animosity between Caesar and the senate. He's on a roll, and like a political game of Scrabble, you might say that Caesar is a consul who counts double. By the way, what's become of the other consul elected at the same time as Caesar? You know—Bibulus? His name is not heard much on Roman lips. Intimidated by Caesar's battering-ram approach, he wastes no time barricading himself at home and doesn't go out. The Romans conclude that the dual office of consul is really held by "Julius and Caesar." Toward the end of the term, the senate must choose the place where the consul will be sent to serve as proconsul. Will the senate try to get back at Caesar for his behavior toward them? You bet. The senate proposes to stick him in some out-of-the-way provinces in a forgotten corner of Italy. Fortunately, the *Lex Vatinia*—whose name comes from the tribune who proposed it—gives Caesar governorship of Cisalpine Gaul and Illyria (Yugoslavia), as well as three legions. The senate, in a showdown with popular opinion, caves in and adds not only Transalpine Gaul but a fourth legion as well!

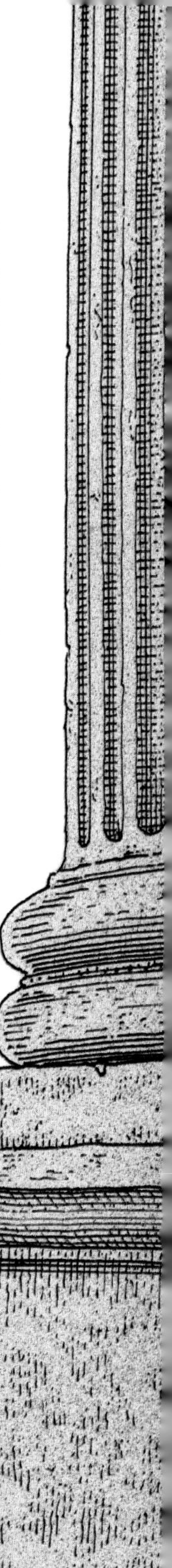

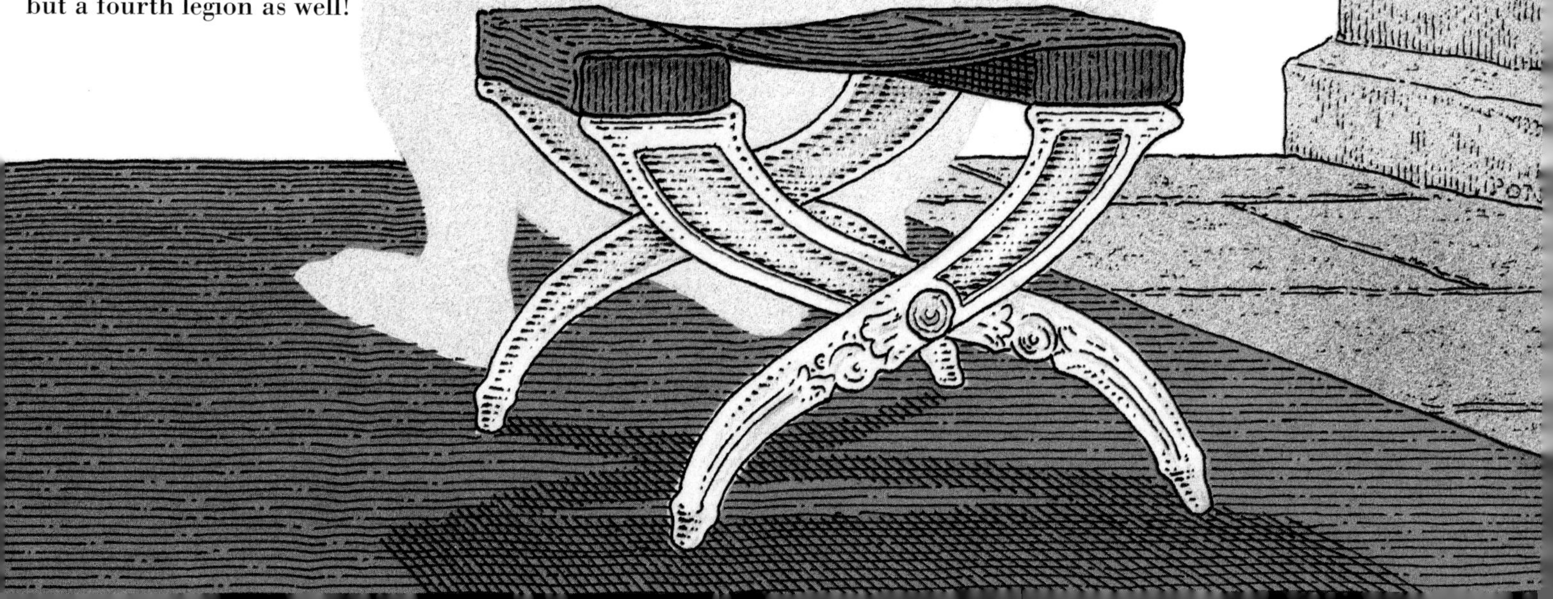

1. Equites belong to the equestrian order, situated between the nobility and the common people. This social class is made up of newly wealthy landowners, businessmen, and bankers. They are called knights because they are rich enough to buy themselves horses for their military service. Some equites choose political careers—Marius, Pompey, and Cicero, for example. They are called "new men" because they are the first in their family to go into politics, long monopolized by the patricians. They wear a gold ring as a symbol of their social class.

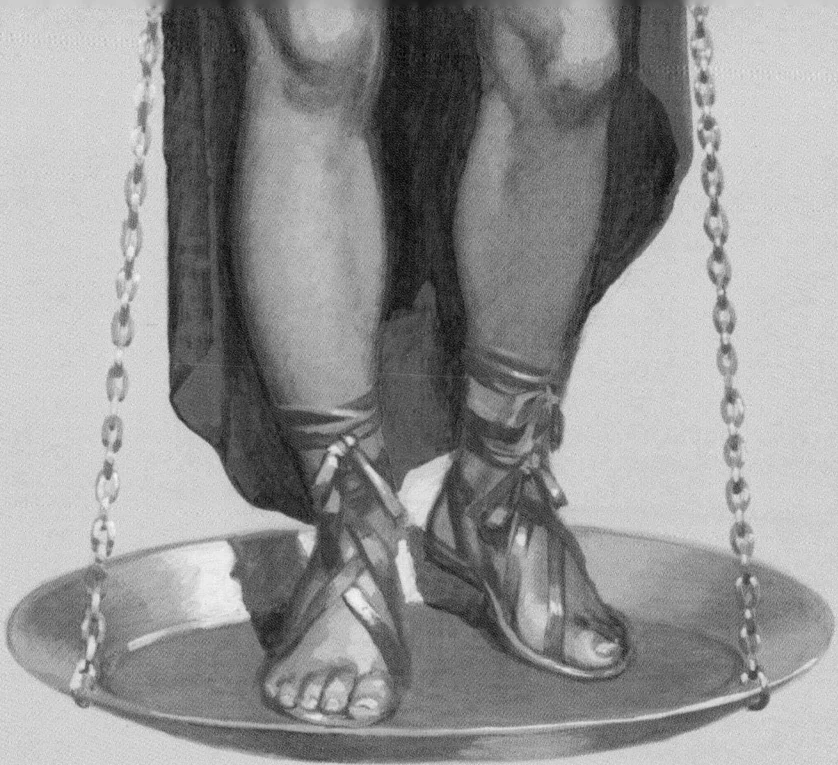

THERE'S NOTHING LIKE MONEY FOR GIVING YOUR CAREER A BOOST

In Rome, everything costs money[1]: friendship, marriage, votes. You need chariots full of money in order to get into politics and to live, because the state pays its elected officials a ridiculously small salary. Every politician must be very generous with the people, throwing them banquets and showering them with money. In return, he expects the people to vote for him in the next elections. In Rome, misers are rare and are poorly regarded: "The little people adore those who spare no expense," said Appian, a Roman historian. Romans don't know about saving. For them, money is meant to be spent, and if it's spent on others, so much the better! Although of noble origin, Caesar's family isn't rolling in sesterces. So Caesar borrows from friends and relatives. The result is that after ten years of politics, he's broke. He doesn't exactly try to hold down his expenses either: during his term as aedile in 65 B.C., according to custom he puts on a combat of 320 pairs of gladiators (gladiators cost an arm and a leg) for the people. All in honor of his father, who has been dead for twenty years. His command in Gaul comes just in time: now he will be able to pay off the 25 million sesterces he owes and even make some money. In Rome, all conquests include total or partial annexation of the territories and the taking of booty. Caesar wants to become wealthy, but he also wants to share the wealth. After a victory, in addition to giving his soldiers part of the spoils, he sometimes allows them to pillage a city, as in the case of Córdoba after the battle of Munda in March 45 B.C. To keep his memory alive at home, he sends money regularly to Rome to his friends and future supporters.

1. Four coins are commonly used in ancient Rome: the *as* (plural, *asses*) is bronze, the *sestertius* ("sesterce") is silver, the *denarius* (plural, *denarii*) is also silver, and the *aureus* is gold.

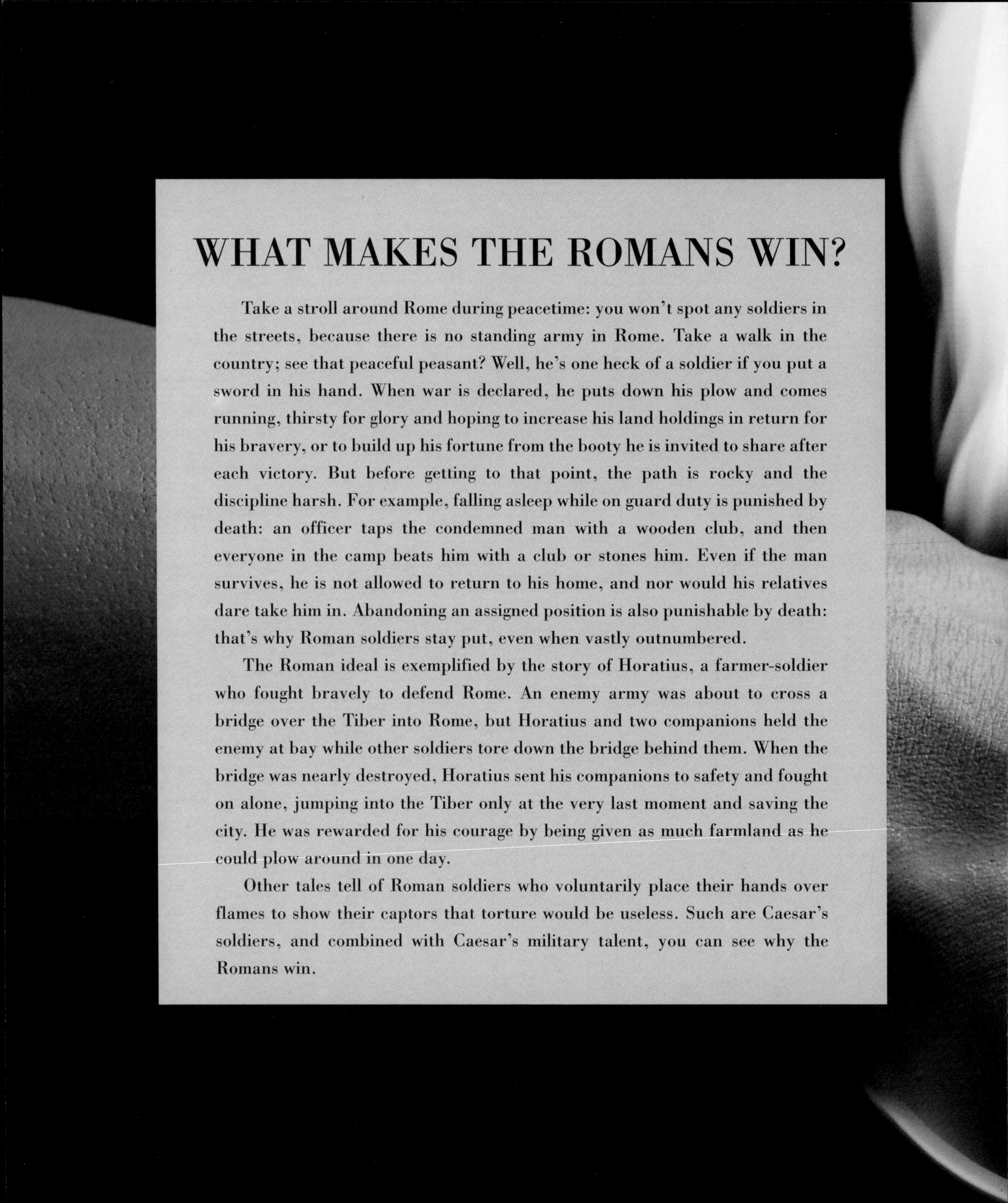

WHAT MAKES THE ROMANS WIN?

Take a stroll around Rome during peacetime: you won't spot any soldiers in the streets, because there is no standing army in Rome. Take a walk in the country; see that peaceful peasant? Well, he's one heck of a soldier if you put a sword in his hand. When war is declared, he puts down his plow and comes running, thirsty for glory and hoping to increase his land holdings in return for his bravery, or to build up his fortune from the booty he is invited to share after each victory. But before getting to that point, the path is rocky and the discipline harsh. For example, falling asleep while on guard duty is punished by death: an officer taps the condemned man with a wooden club, and then everyone in the camp beats him with a club or stones him. Even if the man survives, he is not allowed to return to his home, and nor would his relatives dare take him in. Abandoning an assigned position is also punishable by death: that's why Roman soldiers stay put, even when vastly outnumbered.

The Roman ideal is exemplified by the story of Horatius, a farmer-soldier who fought bravely to defend Rome. An enemy army was about to cross a bridge over the Tiber into Rome, but Horatius and two companions held the enemy at bay while other soldiers tore down the bridge behind them. When the bridge was nearly destroyed, Horatius sent his companions to safety and fought on alone, jumping into the Tiber only at the very last moment and saving the city. He was rewarded for his courage by being given as much farmland as he could plow around in one day.

Other tales tell of Roman soldiers who voluntarily place their hands over flames to show their captors that torture would be useless. Such are Caesar's soldiers, and combined with Caesar's military talent, you can see why the Romans win.

PRESENTS

EIGHTEEN MILES ON FOOT, EACH AND EVERY DAY

War is an ordinary occurrence in the Rome of the age of Caesar; it's peace that's extraordinary. Every citizen is a potential soldier, the draft age is between seventeen and forty-six. Noncitizens, slaves, and freedmen are automatically excluded from the army because only citizens have this privilege. The cost of a soldier's weapons is subtracted from his pay, but the state provides his food.

Caesar's uncle General Marius opens the Roman army to people who don't own land, attracting many volunteers and making it a professional army.

When the red flag flies over the citadel, men know that they have thirty days to show up at Rome's Campus Martius (the "field of Mars," god of war), where the *dilectus*, or mustering of troops, takes place. Soldiers from each tribe are selected by lottery until the number desired by the consuls has been reached. Then, twenty-four military tribunes select and divide the men into the different legions. A legion has about 4,200 men (subdivided into centuries of 100 men or maniples of 120) plus a cavalry corps. Four legions are usually drafted for a total of about 17,000 men.

The soldiers take an oath before the tribunes, who in turn take an oath before the general. Caesar does away with these intermediary steps and attaches the soldiers directly to himself. This will turn out to be one of the keys to his extraordinary success. Caesar also doubles the soldiers wages to 6 *asses*[1] (12 *asses* for a centurion, the leader of a century).

Military campaigns usually take place from April to October.

1. Under Caesar, a *sestertius* (silver) is worth four *asses*, a *denarius* (silver) is worth four sesterces, and an *aureus* (gold) is worth twenty-five *denarii*.

THE TEN (MILITARY) COMMANDMENTS

Legio expedita!
Attention!
Signa inferre!
Forward!
Praege!
March!
Certo gradu!
Keep in step!
Concursu!
Charge!
Incitato gradu!
Double time!
Signa statuere!
Halt!
Infestis pilis!
Take aim!
Ad gladios!
To arms!
Agmen torquere!
Change direction!

EACH SOLDIER HAS HIS EQUIPMENT
Soldiers are grouped into types according to age and social standing, and each type uses different weapons.
- *the cavalryman: spear, sword, shield;*
- *the legionary: body armor of leather straps with shoulder pieces to protect the upper body, metal helmet, which also protects the neck and cheeks, curved shield, short sword, javelin (over six feet long);*
- *the* velites *(the youngest): short sword, round shield, leather helmet, javelin or spear;*
- *the* hastati *(spearmen): sword, oblong shield, spear.*

Roman soldiers often adapt the best weapons from their defeated enemies, such as the coat of mail from Gaul or the two-edged sword from Spain.

THE LEGION ON THE BATTLEFIELD
The infantry is in the middle, the cavalry on the flanks. Once the javelins are thrown, hand-to-hand combat begins. The 1,200 hastati, *or spearmen, are in the front line, then 1,200* principes, *or older men, in the second, and the 600* triari, *or javelin throwers, in the third and last line. The* velites, *the youngest soldiers, are spread throughout the three ranks. The whole group moves by divisions of 120 men called maniples.*

EIGHTEEN MILES ON FOOT, EVERY DAY
In general, a soldier covers over eighteen miles each day, with about 60 pounds on his back (including his equipment, food, weapons, and tools for building the camp) and his helmet slung around his neck.

THE TORTOISE FORMATION, A ROMAN TACTIC
During sieges, the soldiers form tight ranks, holding their shields above their heads like a roof to protect them from projectiles.

BATAVIANS
ADUATUCI
MENAPII
MORINI
EBURONES
ATREBATES
NERVII
CONDRUSI
AMBIANI
VIROMANDUI
TREVERI
BELLOVACI
REMI
SUESSIONES
VELIOCASSES
VENELLI
SILVANECTES
MEDIOMATRICI
LEXOVII
VIDUCASSES
MELDI
AULERICI
EBUROVICES
ABRINCATUENS
PARISII
LEUCI
OSISMI
CORIOSOLITES
AULERICI
CENOMANI
CARNUTES
TRICASSES
REDONES
SENONES
VENETI
DIABLINTES
VELLAVII
RAURICI
MANDUBII
ANDES
AEDUI
NAMNETES
LINGON
TURONI
SEQUANI
BITURIGES CUBI
PICTONES
AMBARRI
LEMOVICES
SANTONI
SEGUSIAVI
ALLOBROGES
ARVERNI
BITURIGES
VIVISCI
PETROCORII
VELLAVII
HELVII
CADURCI
VOCONTI
BOII
NITIOBROGES
GABALI
COCOSATES
ELUSATES
RUTENES
TARBELLI
SOTIATES
AUSCI
SIBULATES
VOLCAE
TECTOSAGES
VOLCAE
ARECOMICI
CONVENES
SORDONES

CAESAR, ONE OF HISTORY'S FIRST WAR CORRESPONDENTS

The Bituriges, Carnutes, Nervii, Sequani, and Bellovaci are only a few of the tribes inhabiting the distant land of Gaul, known for its rain and its dark forests. The Gauls came to Rome and sacked it in 390 B.C., but no Romans before Caesar have ever gone beyond the Roman province of Narbonensis in Gaul. Gaul is comprised of sixty or so tribes of different customs and habits. Its territory is rich and covered with forests. Two regions, Celtic Gaul in the center, and Belgian Gaul to the north, are part of independent Gaul (*Gallia Comata*). Each tribe has its assembly, its army, and its ambassadors. In times of war, the weakest tribes pay a *tributum* ("tribute," but really a ransom) to the strongest ones, with hostages as a security deposit! In contrast to Italy, which is about to be unified under Roman rule, Gaul appears to be a vast, disorganized land. After his term as consul, Caesar dreams of a large command, and he gets it. He doesn't particularly want a big war, but he gets that, too. The eight years of his conquests in Gaul allow him to acquire wealth and glory. He has certainly gotten a lot more than he asked for. The first campaign seems purely defensive. The Helvetii, driven by their leader Orgetorix, want to move to Saintes near the Atlantic coast by crossing the Roman province of Narbonensis. Caesar sees this as a threat to Tolosa (Toulouse) and moves against them. He wins the battle at Bibracte in June 58 B.C. Then comes war with the Suebi, a Germanic people led by Ariovistus, a king and former ally of Rome about whom the Sequani and Aedui, neighboring tribes, are always complaining. Caesar calls a meeting with the king. During the discussion, Ariovistus' men start to throw stones at the Romans. Caesar cannot tolerate such an affront and declares war. The Suebi are repulsed beyond the Rhine after being defeated near Mulhouse. "The Helvetii, the Suebi were undoubtedly courageous, but what is bravery against an army disciplined and constituted like the Roman army? There is thus nothing extraordinary in the successes obtained by Caesar in this campaign, which, however, does not diminish the glory he merits" (Napoleon, *Summary of the Wars of Caesar*). All during 57 B.C., Caesar battles the Suessiones and the Nervii, Belgian tribes. In April 56 B.C., Caesar goes to Lucca in Cisalpine Gaul to renew the Triumvirate. His command in Gaul is extended five more years. Between 56 and 54 B.C., Caesar leaves on a reconnaissance mission to Germania and the island of Britain. His lieutenants vanquish the peoples near the Gulf of Morbihan, the Veneti and the Venelli, and the Sotiates in Aquitania. In 55 B.C., Caesar massacres the Usipetes and the Tenctheri, northern peoples. Then it's the Belgian tribes' turn to revolt, first the Treveri, then the Eburones. The Eburones, led by Ambiorix, cause the loss of more than one Roman legion (over 5,500 men), the heaviest loss of Roman lives during the entire Gallic War. On January 23, 52 B.C., the massacre of Roman merchants in the city of Cenabum (Orleans) marks the general uprising in Celtic Gaul: Senones, Parisii, Pictones, Cadurci, Aulerci, Bituriges, and Arverni join under the command of the young (he's only thirty) leader of the Arverni, Vercingetorix—the ardent, intelligent, and daring defender of Gallic freedom against Roman tyranny. Caesar takes Gorgobina, Vellaunodunum, Noviodunum, Cenabum, and Avaricum before retreating from the *oppidum* (fortified settlement) of Gergovia in June 52 B.C.

CAESAR AS SEEN BY CAESAR

In his Gallic War, *the Roman commander reveals himself a skilled historian. His work will be a best-seller over the centuries. It is intended as a manifesto of propaganda, easily accessible to the reader, so that the Roman people would be sympathetic to his difficult war with the Gauls. He calls this work a commentary, meaning it is not a serious "history" but more like a commander's dispatches or memoranda, enlivened by speeches and letters exchanged between Caesar and the senate. Caesar speaks of himself in the third person, which allows him to write his name hundreds of times. He exaggerates the numbers of the enemy and discreetly leaves out certain defeats; but he doesn't just talk about military operations. He describes many geographic locations and tells us something about the customs of the Gauls.*

FIELD CAMP

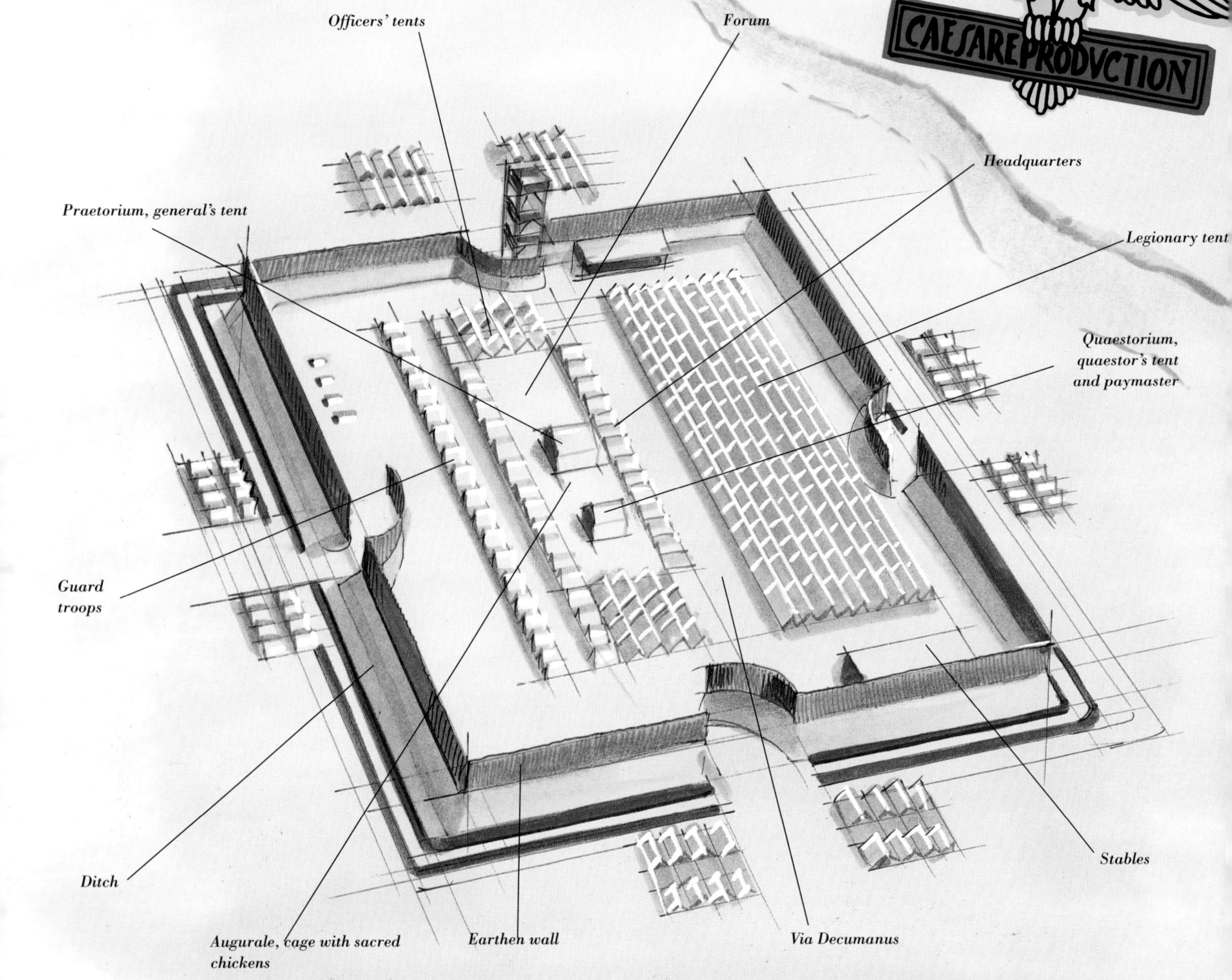
Officers' tents
Forum
Headquarters
Praetorium, general's tent
Legionary tent
Quaestorium, quaestor's tent and paymaster
Guard troops
Stables
Ditch
Augurale, cage with sacred chickens
Earthen wall
Via Decumanus

To survive, a soldier must fight, and he fights everywhere: in Italy, Gaul, Thrace, Egypt, Spain. To rest, he must work. Once the fighting is over, armed with a pick-ax and a shovel, he digs, cuts, builds—he is setting up camp. The camp, or *castrum*, is one of the characteristics of the Roman army. One kind of camp is the field, or temporary, camp, which is set up and dismantled daily. The site for a camp is chosen for its proximity to a meadow and a source of water. All camps are built according to the same model. The square or rectangular site is built within an enclosure with four gates and is surrounded by one or more defensive ditches. The camp is lined up along two perpendicular axes: the *cardo*, or north-south, and the *decumanus*, or east-west. At the intersection of the *cardo* and the *decumanus* are the general's tent and a camp-sized forum. A workshop repairs and makes weapons as well as bricks and tiles. A camp holds two legions, or over 8,000 men, and measures 1,800 by 2,600 feet. Soldiers in the same unit sleep according to their order on the battlefield, in leather tents arranged in double rows parallel to the main axes. Discipline in the camp is very strict, and the general has power of life and death over his soldiers. Soldiers eat wheat cakes with bacon and cheese and drink water mixed with vinegar (the same drink will be given to Jesus on the cross).

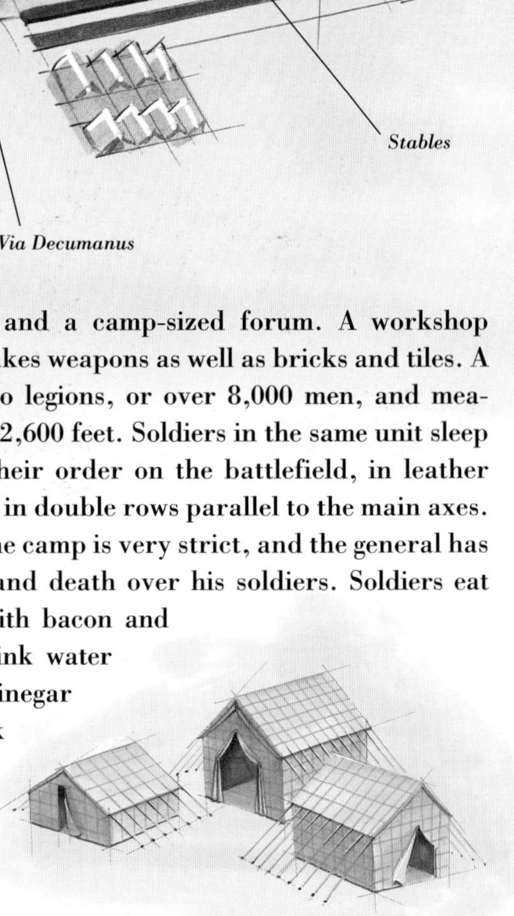

SIEGE CAMP

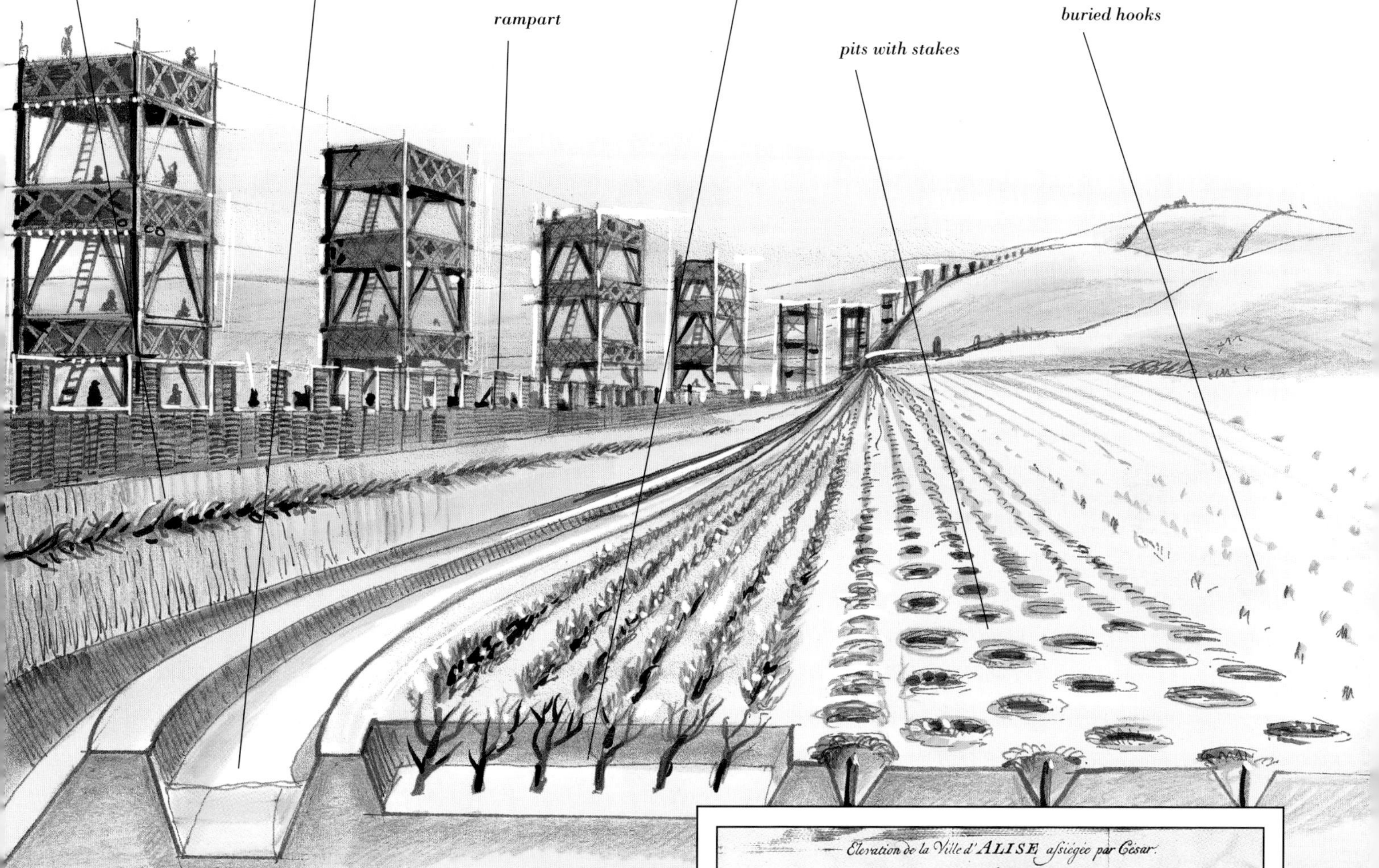

forked branches
trench
rampart
buried branches
pits with stakes
buried hooks

There is also the siege camp, a fortified site built to be held for more than one night. At Alesia, Caesar has his men dig trenches, one filled with water; in front of these they build further defensive rows, one of buried sharpened tree branches, one of pits with sharpened stakes at the bottom, and one of blocks of wood with iron hooks, buried at ground level and barely visible. They stick forked branches in the walls to keep the enemy from climbing up.

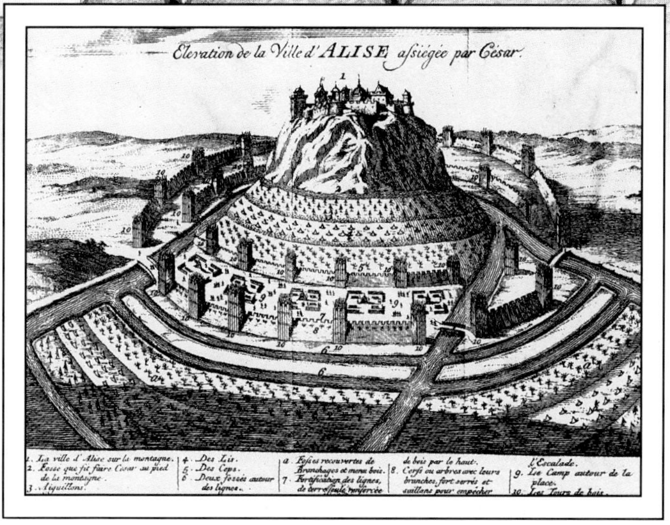

Elevation de la Ville d'ALISE assiégée par César.
1. La ville d'Alise sur la montagne.
2. Fosse que fit faire César au pied de la montagne.
3. Aiguillons.
4. Des Lis.
5. Des Ceps.
6. Deux fossés autour des lignes.
a. Fosses recouvertes de Branchages et menu bois.
7. Fortification des lignes, de terre soule renforcée de bois par le haut.
8. Cerfs ou arbres avec leurs branches, fort serrés et saillans pour empêcher l'Escalade.
9. Le Camp autour de la place.
10. Les Tours de bois.

Seventeenth-century print of Caesar's siege of Alesia.

Poliorcetics, or siegecraft
The Romans have a knack for sieges. They know better than anyone how to dig trenches and use catapults (1), battering rams (2), for breaking down gates, and ballistae (3), which fire heavy rocks.

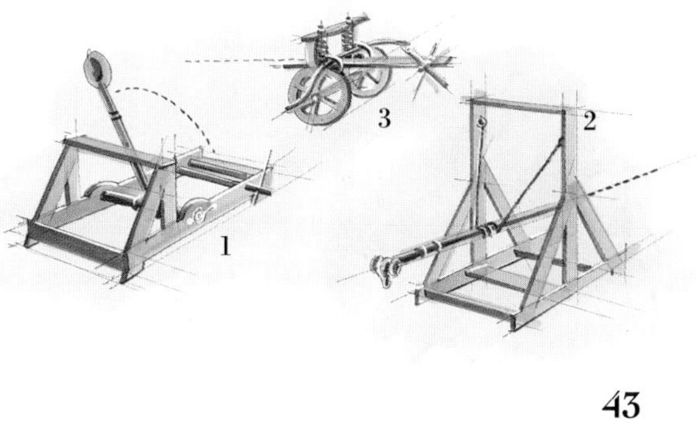

1
2
3

Vercingetorix and his men take refuge in the hill-top fortress of Alesia, near Dijon, in today's eastern France. Caesar besieges the fortress and has his men dig trenches around it, set up towers, and encircle it with a fortified line. On September 27, 52 B.C., Vercingetorix surrenders, throwing down his weapons at Caesar's feet.

ALESIA, LAST OF THE

In June 52 B.C., Caesar is defeated at Gergovia. He loses 700 men. Vercingetorix rallies his victorious troops while Caesar waits for reinforcements, especially cavalrymen.

A few miles from Alesia, Gallic horsemen are the first to attack, but they are crushed and their three chiefs captured, thanks to the Roman cavalry that finally arrives. That same evening in July 52 B.C., Vercingetorix and 80,000 Gauls take refuge in the fortified settlement of Alesia, inhabited by the Mandubii, halfway between the territory of the Lingones, allies of Caesar, and the Aedui, allies of Vercingetorix. Alesia is situated in Alise-Sainte-Reine, about twenty-five miles northeast of Dijon.

Caesar has just joined six of his legions with the four led by his lieutenant Labienus, victor in the battle with the Parisii for their city, Lutece (Paris), some sixty miles from Agendicum (today, the city of Sens).

Arriving near Mount Auxois, on top of which sits Alesia, Caesar, in a glance, analyzes the site and judges its difficulties, which are more numerous for the enemy than for his own troops: Alesia seems more difficult to defend than to lay siege to. His soldiers set to work digging trenches in two defensive lines: a contravallation nine miles long around Alesia to keep Vercingetorix in, and a circumvallation thirteen miles long around that to keep out the Gauls trying to come to their leader's aid. In the area between the two defensive lines the Romans build eight camps joined by twenty-three forts. Within this *vallum* (double trench) the Roman army can maneuver and move about freely. The

GREAT GALLIC BATTLES

Romans have many "propulsion" machines that launch projectiles like stones and flaming arrows. They also strengthen their fortifications by adding sharpened stakes set up in rows to impale anyone attacking the Roman lines. Caesar knows that Vercingetorix cannot hold out for more than a month without food. Soon after the start of the siege, Vercingetorix sends out those who are unable to fight and are thus "useless" mouths to feed, namely old people, women, and children. They try to take refuge with the Romans, but Caesar refuses to let them inside the Roman lines. Gallic reinforcements of 200,000 men arrive and try to break through Caesar's fortifications. The Gauls are beaten back three times. After several skirmishes, the final battle unfolds from noon until midnight. There is total confusion: the fighting takes place on all sides and in every direction, the soldiers of Vercingetorix trying to break through the Roman fortifications from one side, the reinforcements attacking from the other. Watching the enormous battle, Caesar calmly sends men where they are most needed, and his army drives back the attackers. Vercingetorix surrenders on September 27, 52 B.C., and throws down his arms before Caesar. He is made a prisoner. Six years after his capture he will be exhibited at Rome in Caesar's triumph and then executed. The Gallic revolt is not totally put down, but the time of the great battles is past. Only at the end of 51 B.C. will the war in Gaul be officially over. The loss of life is great: the Greek historian Plutarch speaks of a million prisoners and a million dead on the side of the Gauls.

MOVE YOUR FEET, LOSE YOUR SEAT

So where is Pompey, Caesar's main rival, during the Gallic Wars?

In 56 B.C. the Triumvirate is renewed. One year later, the three men vote in a law giving Spain to Pompey for five years, Syria to Crassus for five years, and a five-year extension on Caesar's term as proconsul in Gaul. After the death of Julia in childbirth in September 54 B.C., and the death of Crassus in June 53 B.C., the ties between Caesar and Pompey become severely frayed. Pompey gets chummier with the senate and keeps an eye on Caesar for any false moves. In 53 B.C., anarchy reigns in the streets of Rome, where the opposing gangs of Milo, an *optimate* close to Pompey, and Clodius, a *populare* and friend of Caesar's, are squaring off. On January 20, 52 B.C., Clodius is killed during a scuffle. There is rioting in the streets, and the people burn down the Curia. The next day, the senate gives Pompey full powers to restore order. On February 26, Pompey is named solo consul, in defiance of the laws of the republic. Caesar doesn't do anything about it because he has a deal worked out with Pompey, who promises to get rid of Milo, now condemned to capital punishment and on the lam. While Pompey is the uncontested master of Rome, Caesar is about to enter into battle against Vercingetorix. Pompey takes advantage of the situation to pass laws that are not very favorable to his ex-father-in-law, such as the obligation for Caesar to come in person to Rome to state his intention to run for consul. No more special treatment for the bald one! Then there is quibbling over the date upon which Caesar's term as proconsul ends, because he can run for consul only ten years after the date of his first election. Everyone gets the dates mixed up, and Caesar gets annoyed. From Ravenna, he sends a message to the senate, trying to reach an agreement. Instead, on January 7, 49 B.C., the senate declares Caesar an outlaw.

CAESARE
QUART

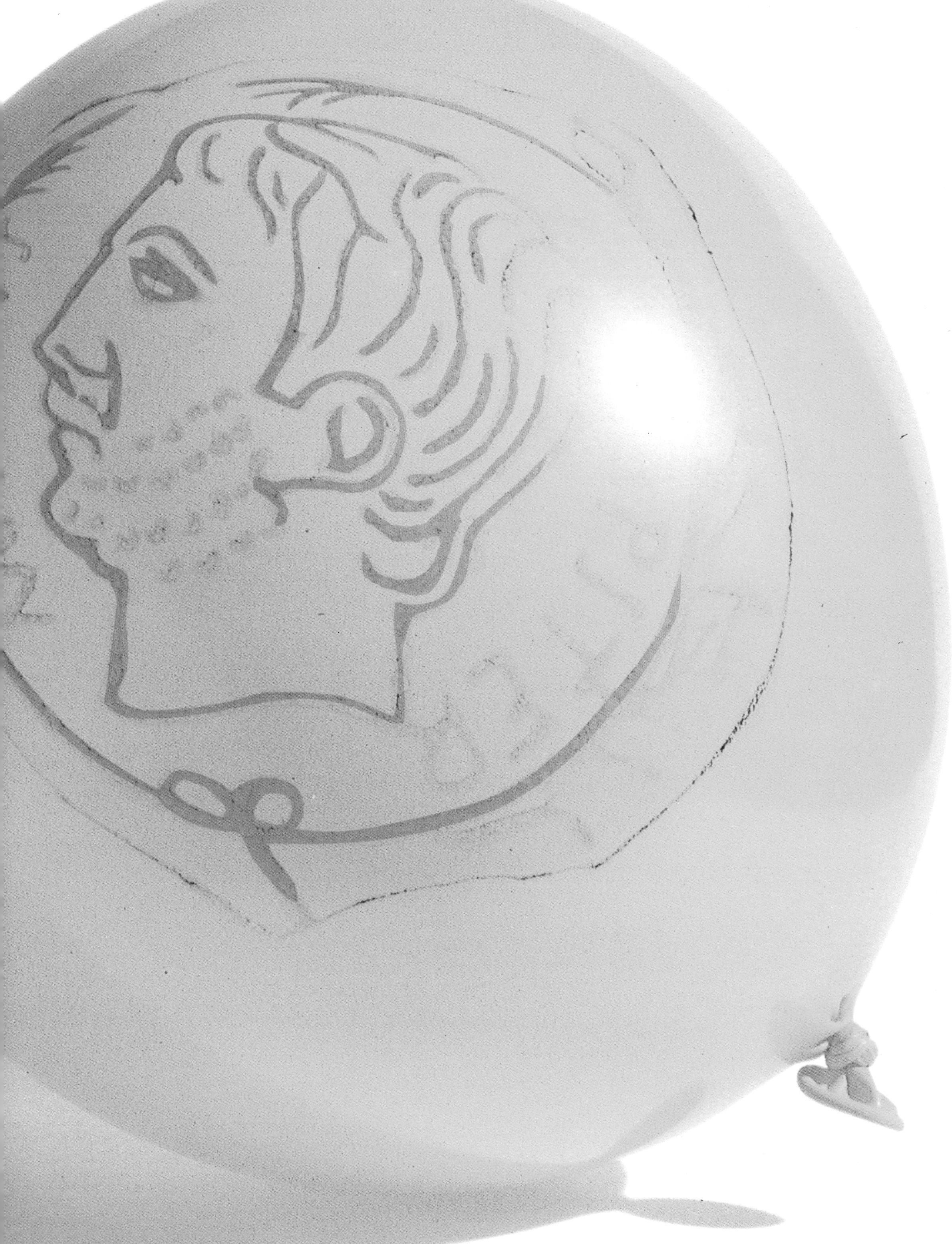

QUART

THE OUTLAW MAKES HIS OWN LAWS

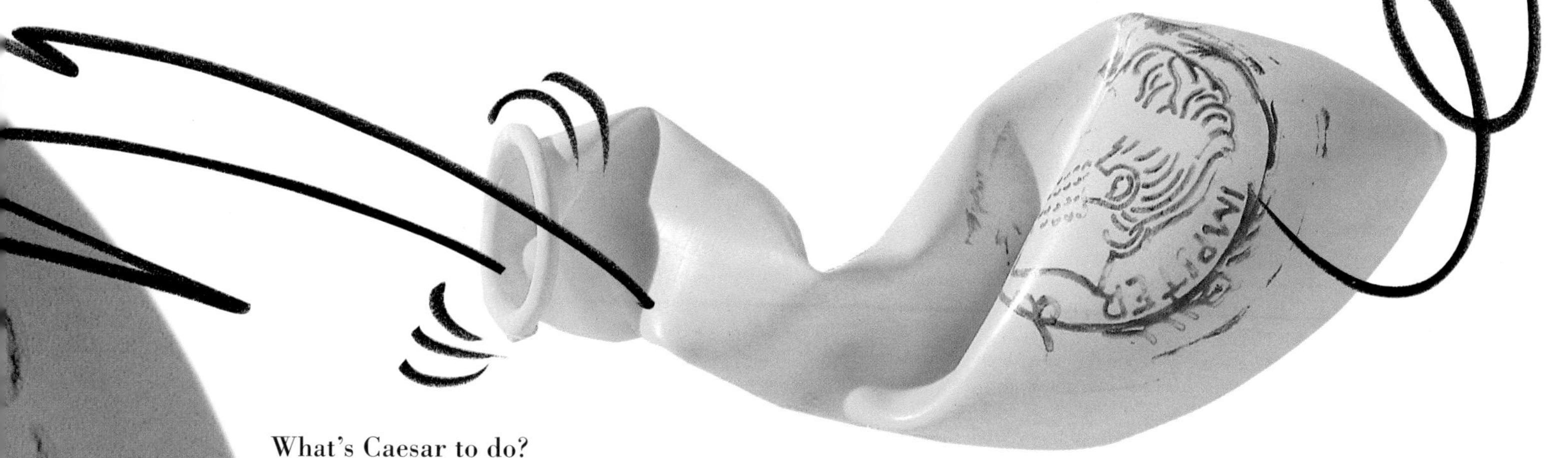

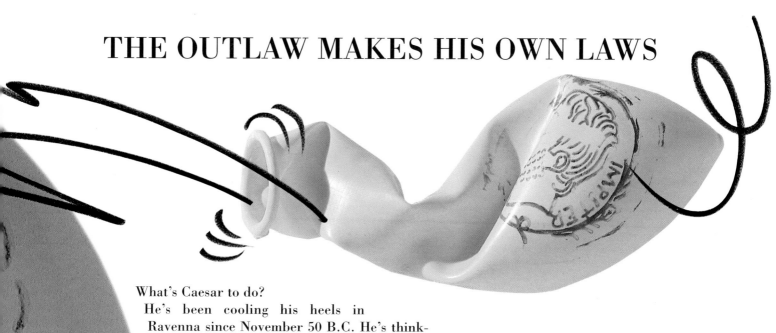

What's Caesar to do? He's been cooling his heels in Ravenna since November 50 B.C. He's thinking of crossing the Rubicon, a small river that flows about twelve miles north of Rimini and forms the border between Cisalpine Gaul (Caesar's province) and Italy. Roman law forbids him to cross the river with his army—no governor may lead his troops outside his province—so what Caesar is contemplating amounts to treason. To cross or not to cross, that is the question! During the night of January 11-12, 49 B.C., he makes up his mind. By crossing the Rubicon, Caesar knows that he is entering into war against the senate and that a civil war will pit him against Pompey. This is why the phrase "to cross the Rubicon" has become famous, meaning to make an irrevocable decision that carries heavy risks. At this moment Caesar coins another famous phrase when he declares, *Iacta alea est,* or "the die is cast." When he arrives in Rome, he finds the senators and Pompey gone. Everyone is in a panic, losing their heads. The place is going to the dogs! Caesar calmly sets about conquering the rest of Italy. It takes him sixty days in all. On February 21, the city of Corfinium capitulates. Caesar shows great clemency, prompting Cicero to write, "What a contrast between Caesar who saves his enemies and Pompey who abandons his friends." Pompey chooses to flee to Greece, where he has planned for men and reserves to be waiting. In a deserted Rome, Caesar peacefully goes about looting the temple of Saturn, which contains the treasury and its 3,000 pounds of gold and 650,000 pounds of silver, before going to Spain to meet the seven legions loyal to Pompey. "I am off to meet an army without a leader [in Spain]; when I return I shall meet a leader without an army" (Caesar, *The Civil War*). On the way, he orders the siege of Marseille, whose gates remain closed to him as a sign of solidarity with Pompey. The city capitulates in October, after six months of siege. Caesar crushes Pompey's legions on August 2, 49 B.C., at Ilerda. The mutiny of Placentia (October 49): some of Caesar's soldiers think they didn't get a large enough share of the booty from Ilerda and make it known. Their general turns the situation around with some well-chosen words. At first he orders every tenth man killed, but softens and orders only the dozen original instigators executed. At the end of November, Caesar returns to Rome and is named dictator—by the people, not the senate—for eleven days and is elected consul for the following year. Early in January 48 B.C., he sails off in pursuit of Pompey, who gets the stuffing beaten out of him on August 9 at Pharsalus in Thessaly. There are 15,000 casualties on the side of the Pompeians. Caesar enters his adversary's camp. He burns Pompey's records without even reading them, then eats the meal prepared for Pompey, who has fled. Before he can even touch Egyptian soil, the fugitive is stabbed and decapitated on September 28 by the men of King Ptolemy XIII, who prefer to side with Caesar. On October 2, when Caesar arrives in Alexandria, Pompey's head and gold equite ring are brought to him on a platter. Caesar "weeps and moans" according to the Greek historian Dio Cassius, but he doesn't forget to send Pompey's ring to Rome as a sign of victory. Pompey's death doesn't end the civil war: his many partisans are renewing their courage and gathering forces after the rout at Pharsalus.

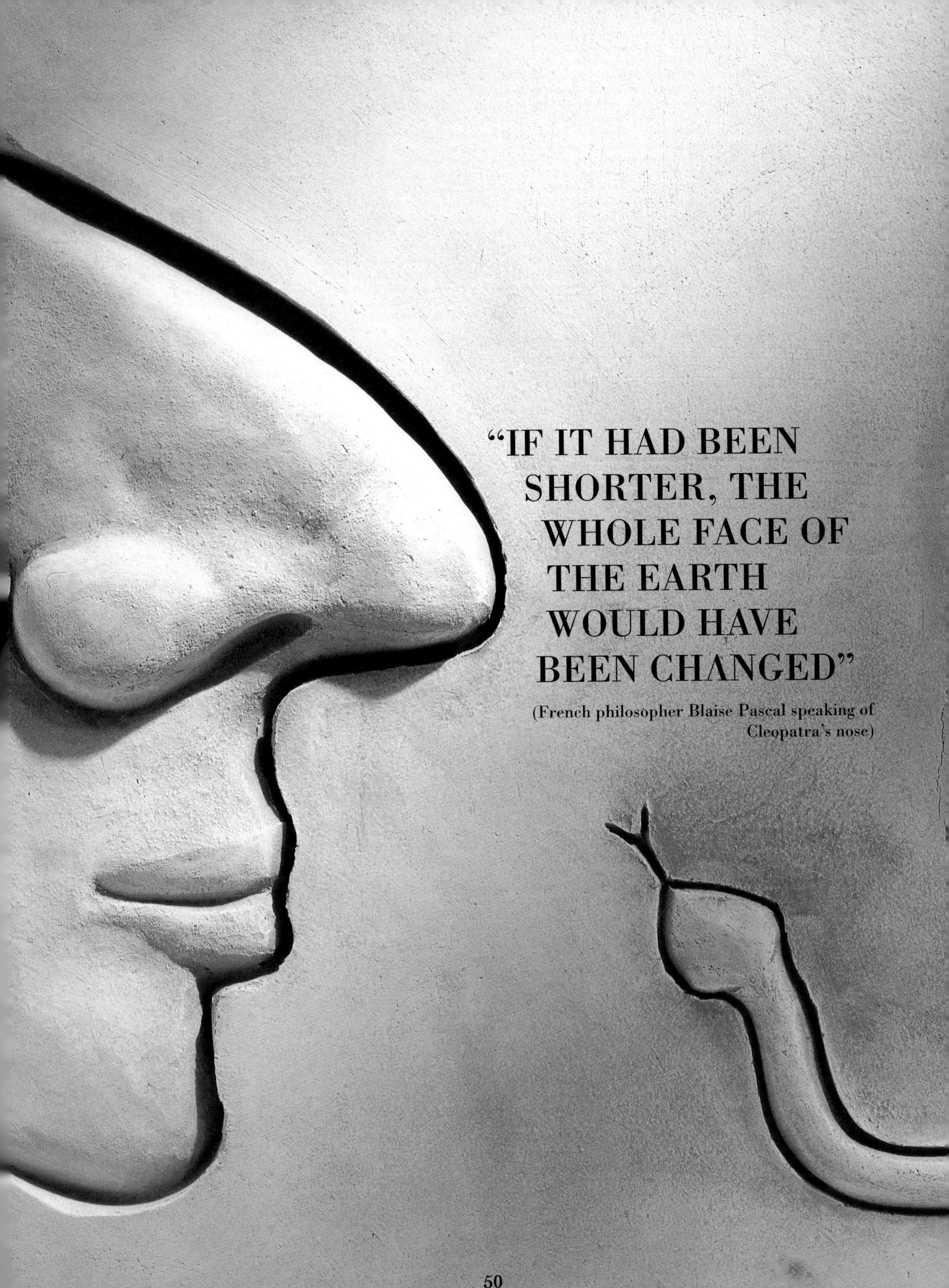

"IF IT HAD BEEN SHORTER, THE WHOLE FACE OF THE EARTH WOULD HAVE BEEN CHANGED"

(French philosopher Blaise Pascal speaking of Cleopatra's nose)

Once he arrives in Alexandria, Caesar appears to take on the role of mediator between the Egyptian king Ptolemy XIII, thirteen years old, and his sister-wife Cleopatra (the seventh to carry that name), who after a disagreement with her brother had fled to Syria. Cleopatra wants to plead her case before Caesar, and she comes up with a brilliant plan: she has herself rolled up in a rug and delivered to the palace to meet the bald seducer. Caesar falls under the spell of this twenty-year-old woman (he is fifty-four) who is gracious, cultivated, intelligent, and every bit as ambitious as he is. Ptolemy's general Achillas wants war and orders his 22,000 foot soldiers to march on Alexandria. Caesar and his 6,000 soldiers are besieged in the city. During maneuvers, fire ships intending to set fire to the royal fleet (to prevent Achillas from fleeing) accidentally set Alexandria's famous library ablaze: 400,000 works go up in smoke. The final battle of Alexandria on March 27, 47 B.C., marks a victory for Caesar: 20,000 Egyptians, including the king, are dead. Caesar marries off his new mistress to the king's (and Cleopatra's) younger brother, Ptolemy XIV, then proceeds to take her on a cruise up the Nile aboard the royal boat. Their two-month itinerary includes visits to the pyramids of Cheops, Chephren and Mycerinus, white-walled Memphis, the porticoes and obelisks of Heracleopolis, and the temples of Luxor and Aswan.

Further conquests await Caesar in Asia. Cleopatra is now queen of Egypt. She leaves Alexandria for Rome, where she will live until Caesar is assassinated in 44 B.C., after which she returns home. So ends the story of the bald seducer and the "serpent of the Nile," as the Romans call her. Many questions have been asked about Cesarion, the presumed son of Caesar and Cleopatra. The child is not mentioned in his will. Some think that he is the son of Mark Antony, who will succeed Caesar in the queen's bed. In September 31 B.C., at the battle of Actium, Mark Antony is beaten by Octavian. He then hears the rumor that Cleopatra has committed suicide. Unable to cope with both a military defeat and the loss of his mistress, Mark Antony kills himself. The rumor, however, was false; Cleopatra is alive—at least until she learns of Mark Antony's death, for then she bares her breast to an asp's fatal bite.

CAESAR FINISHES AHEAD IN THE MEDITERRANEAN AND

45
RO
46

Caesar leaves for Asia to fight against Pharnaces, son of Mithradates. Pharnaces wants to take back the territories that Pompey seized from his father in 64 B.C. *Veni, vidi, vici* ("I came, I saw, I conquered"): in three words, Caesar sums up the battle of Zela, during which he crushes Pharnaces on August 2, 47 B.C. Caesar mocks Pompey's exploits of twenty years ago: "Fortunate Pompey, here are the enemies whose defeat won you the name Great" (Pompey had crushed Mithradates, causing people to address him as *Magnus*).

The civil war flares up again, this time in Africa, where the sons of Pompey, Gnaeus and Sextus, followed by supporters of their deceased father, have gathered. In spite of reinforcements for the Pompeians from the

LAST THREE LEGS OF THE TOUR DE
WINS THE CIVIL WAR

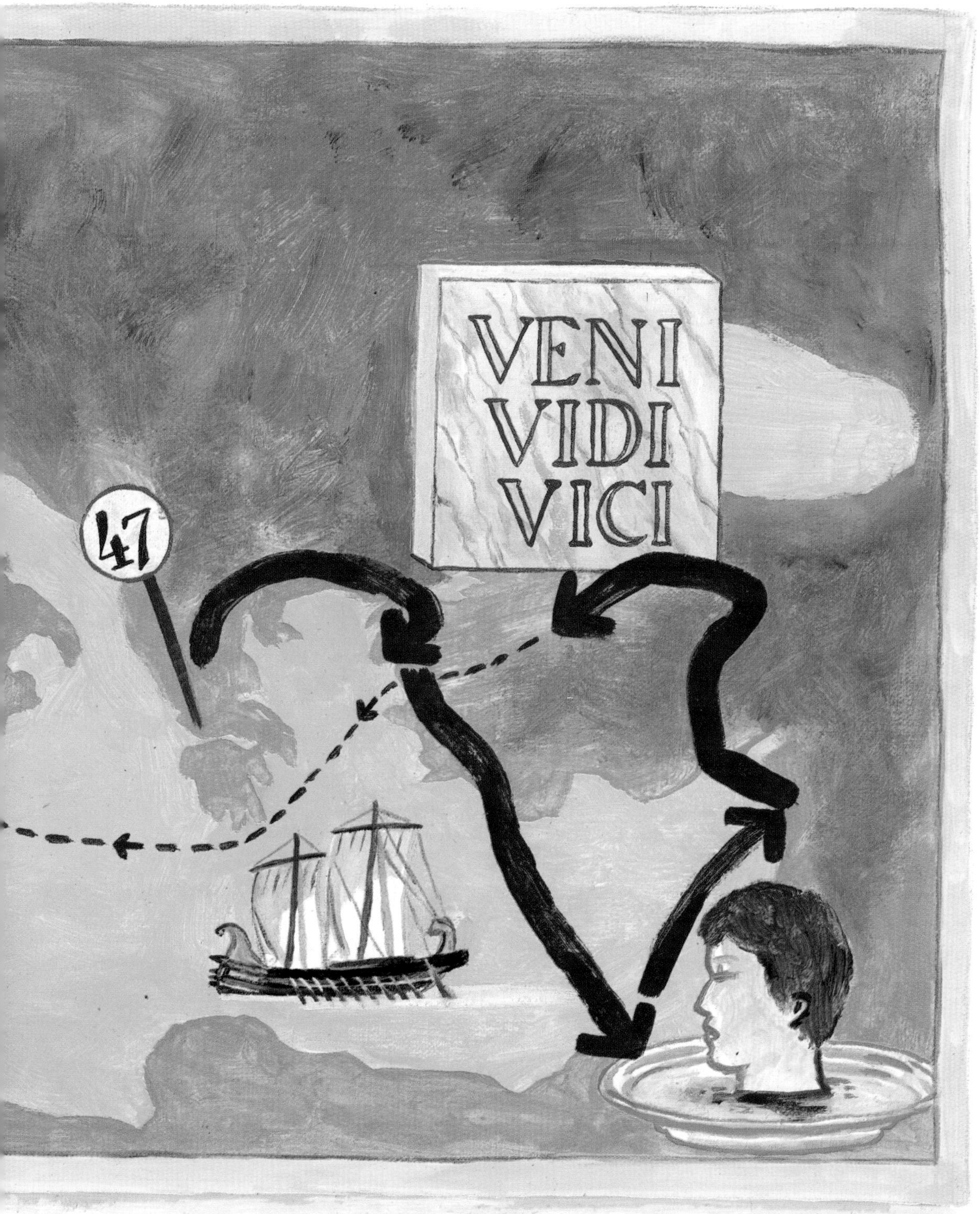
VENI
VIDI
VICI
47

king of Mauritania, Juba I, Caesar is once again victorious: he wins the battle of Thapsus in Tunisia on April 6, 46 B.C. Cato of Utica, upon hearing this news, commits suicide, stabbing himself in the abdomen with his sword. His entrails fall out but are put back in by a doctor. Once Cato is alone, he rips out his stitches and this time dies for good in order to escape the death of the republic, which to Cato is what Caesar symbolizes. It is at Munda, about 20 miles south of Córdoba, on March 17, 45 B.C., that the last part of the civil war is played out. Caesar wins again. Gnaeus is decapitated, Sextus flees. Caesar is at last going to enjoy supreme power.

He returns to Rome. He doesn't suspect that he has only one year to live . . .

ROME RIDES

"Every day, the life of the Roman people is the plaything of the seas and storms." (Ovid)

Rome is fed by surrounding farms, but many products also come to her by sea: wheat from Egypt and Sicily, pepper and other spices from Asia. Maritime routes[1] are taken as often as those on land, but they are not without dangers (storms and pirates) and are navigable for only part of the year: between the months of March and November the Mediterranean is *mare clausum*, meaning it is closed to commerce because of weather conditions. An excellent swimmer, Caesar loves the water, but since he doesn't have his own fleet, he must have ships built on location during conquests or else seize his enemy's fleet. During the war in Gaul, Caesar travels as far as England. He also crosses the Rhine and sails on the Rhone, neither of which has ever been done by a Roman general. Since her victory in the battle of the Aegates (the Aegadian Isles) in 241 B.C. (the end of the First Punic War between Carthage and Rome), Rome has been mistress of the Mediterranean. The Romans even name it *mare nostrum* ("our sea")! Like the Greeks, the Romans quickly prove to be seafaring people. In war, they use *naves*: 165-foot-long galleys (ships with oars) with one sail. It goes without saying that the rowers are slaves who live in deplorable conditions. For trade, cargo ships with sails are used. They look more imposing with their wider decks and deep, curved hulls. The Mediterranean is a veritable pirates' nest. In 64 B.C., Pompey receives an extraordinary three-year command to wipe them out. To his credit, he accomplishes his mission in only six months. Once in power, Caesar plans two big water projects. They will never be carried out, and for good reason: he wants to divert the Tiber River and drain the marshes surrounding Rome!

1. Principal routes:
Roman ships travel an average of 9 knots, or about 6 miles, an hour, about one-third the speed of today's ships.
Alexandria-Marseille: 30 days; Narbonne-Alexandria: 20 days; Pozzuoli-Alexandria: 9 days; Ostia-Narbonne: 3 days.

THE WAVES

rireme, first century B.C.

ACTION NEWS TEAM LIVE COVERAGE

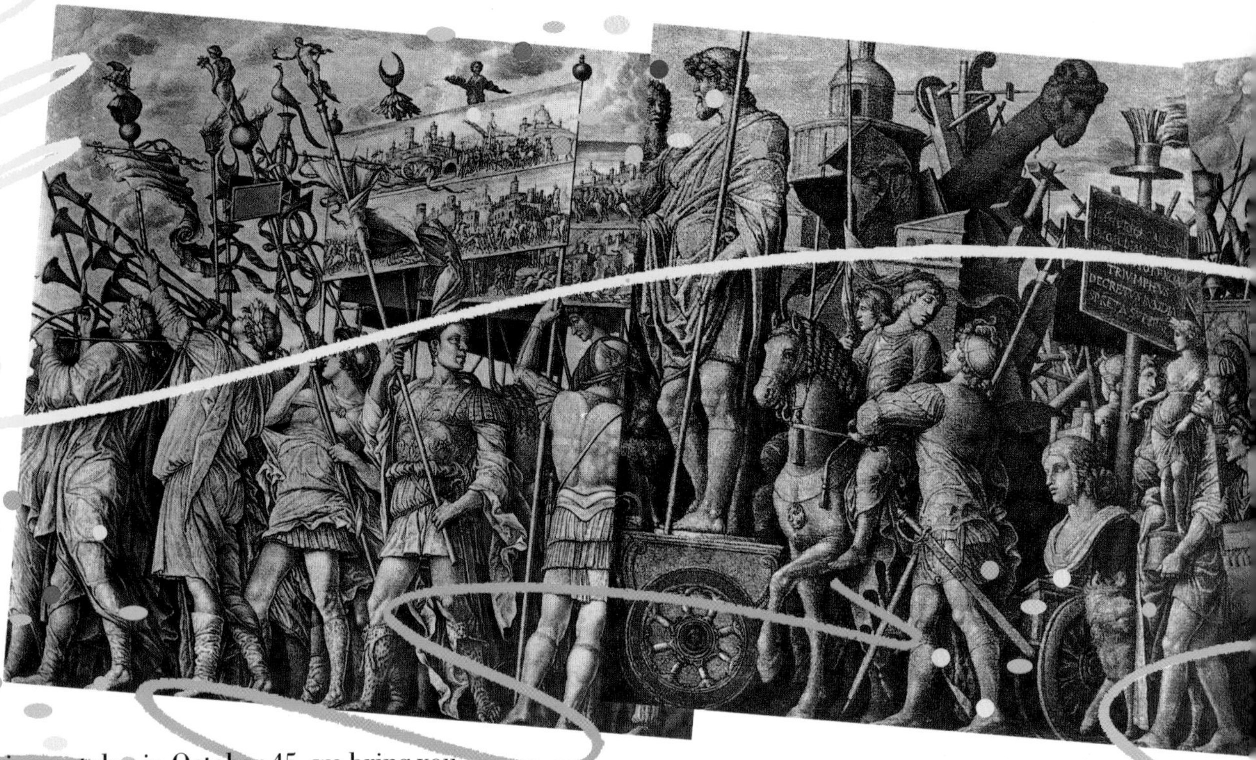

"Today, on this great day in October 45, we bring you to the fifth triumph of our greatest *imperator* Gaius Julius Caesar, he who has conquered Gaul.... The whole city is buzzing with excitement, there are free shows and concerts going on at every street corner.

"I can feel the excitement of the crowd growing—they've been waiting out here under awnings that have been set up to prevent sunstroke—I just got a glimpse of the magistrates leading the procession....The parade route goes all the way across town to the temple of Jupiter on the Capitoline Hill, along the *Via Sacra*, or Sacred Way.

"Just behind the magistrates, I can make out mountains of gold coins and jewelry heaped on the wagons: those must be the spoils. Now the soldiers are marching past to the sound of a fanfare. Some of them are carrying signs with names on them—names of rivers, cities, countries—all the places conquered by Rome. We've heard he'd be driving four white horses, and it's true: here he is in all his glory, Caesar, enthroned on a chariot drawn by four white horses. In my opinion, this is his most magnificent triumph to date, and I think it won't be the last....

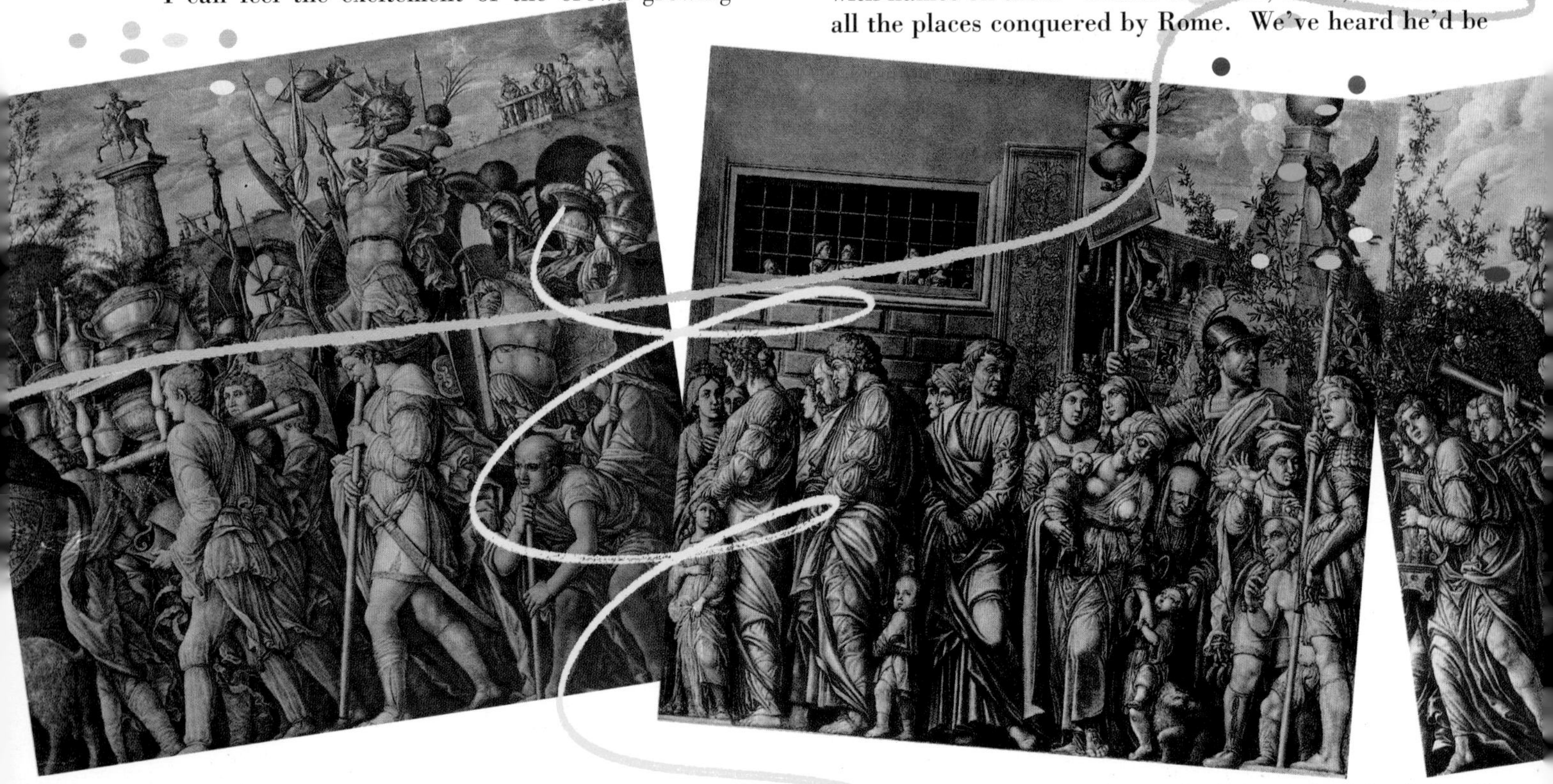

"Rumor has it that a sumptuous buffet is going to be served to the Roman people this afternoon, along with the

OF CAESAR'S TRIUMPHANT VICTORY PARADE

finest wines. My sources tell me that six thousand moray eels, fresh from sea-fed tanks, are on the menu!... I'm also told that Caesar is going to distribute 400 sesterces to each Roman citizen, as well as oil and wheat! I'd say that with the fortune he's amassed, Caesar can well afford it!

"We're coming up to the end of the procession now—this is where they display the prisoners. The most famous one, of course, is Vercingetorix, leader of the Gauls, and here he comes now, chained to his cart. There's Arsinoe—as you may know, she got in the way of her sister, Cleopatra, whom I believe will also be making an appearance today...

"Now, wait a minute, what's this? Here's an animal with the longest legs and neck I've ever seen, spots all over, too. I've never seen such a tall creature! I've just been told that it's called a giraffe—and it's the first time that the people of Rome have ever seen one. It certainly is the first time for me . . . To top it all off, Caesar has had an artificial lake dug at the Campus Martius, and they're going to reenact the battle of Alexandria, complete with 2,000 men!

"Please tune in at eleven for a complete recap. Now back to you at the studio."

VENI VIDI VICI

EVERYONE HAS AN OPINION ABOUT

Beware of that boy with the loose clothes.
Sulla

As the sanctuary dedicated to the Dioscuri, Castor and Pollux, is never called anything but the temple of Castor, the games given by Caesar and Bibulus are never anything but the games of Caesar.
Bibulus

Let us accept this as a sign from the Gods and follow where they beckon, in vengeance on our double-dealing enemies. The die is cast.
Caesar before crossing the Rubicon

Are you not ashamed to give in? As for me, I prefer to kill myself right now than to fall, at the age of fifty-five, to the power of this callow youth, and tarnish even one day of the glory that so many exploits have brought me.
Caesar to his soldiers before Munda

CAESAR, EVEN CAESAR HIMSELF

What a contrast between Caesar who saves his enemies and Pompey who abandons his friends.
Cicero

Africa, I have tight hold of you.
(Caesar setting foot on African soil)

Go on, my friend, and fear nothing; you carry Caesar and his fortune in your boat.
(Caesar, disguised as a slave, to a ship's master during a storm)

My mother, today you will see me either high priest or an exile.
(Caesar to his mother upon leaving to learn the results of his election to the office of Pontifex Maximus, for which he bought most of the votes)

I am Caesar and not king.
(Caesar)

Men believe what they desire.
(Caesar, from *The Civil War*)

Every woman's man and every man's woman

Home we bring our bald seducer;
Romans, lock your wives away!
Caesar's soldiers

DOWNTIME

5:00: Jentaculum *(breakfast of fruit, bread, and cheese) with Calpurnia (his wife).*

6:00: Mail (People write a lot in Rome. The main writing instrument is a wood tablet covered with wax on which a question is inscribed on the flip side, the top side left for the recipient's response.)

7:00: Meeting with Brutus and Cassius (his future assassins).

8:00: Drop in on Cleo at her place. (She has been living in Rome for some time but returns to Egypt when Caesar dies.)

9:00: Present a rogatio *(a bill) to the senate on the distribution of wheat to the poor.*

10:00: Visit the construction site with the architects of my Forum.

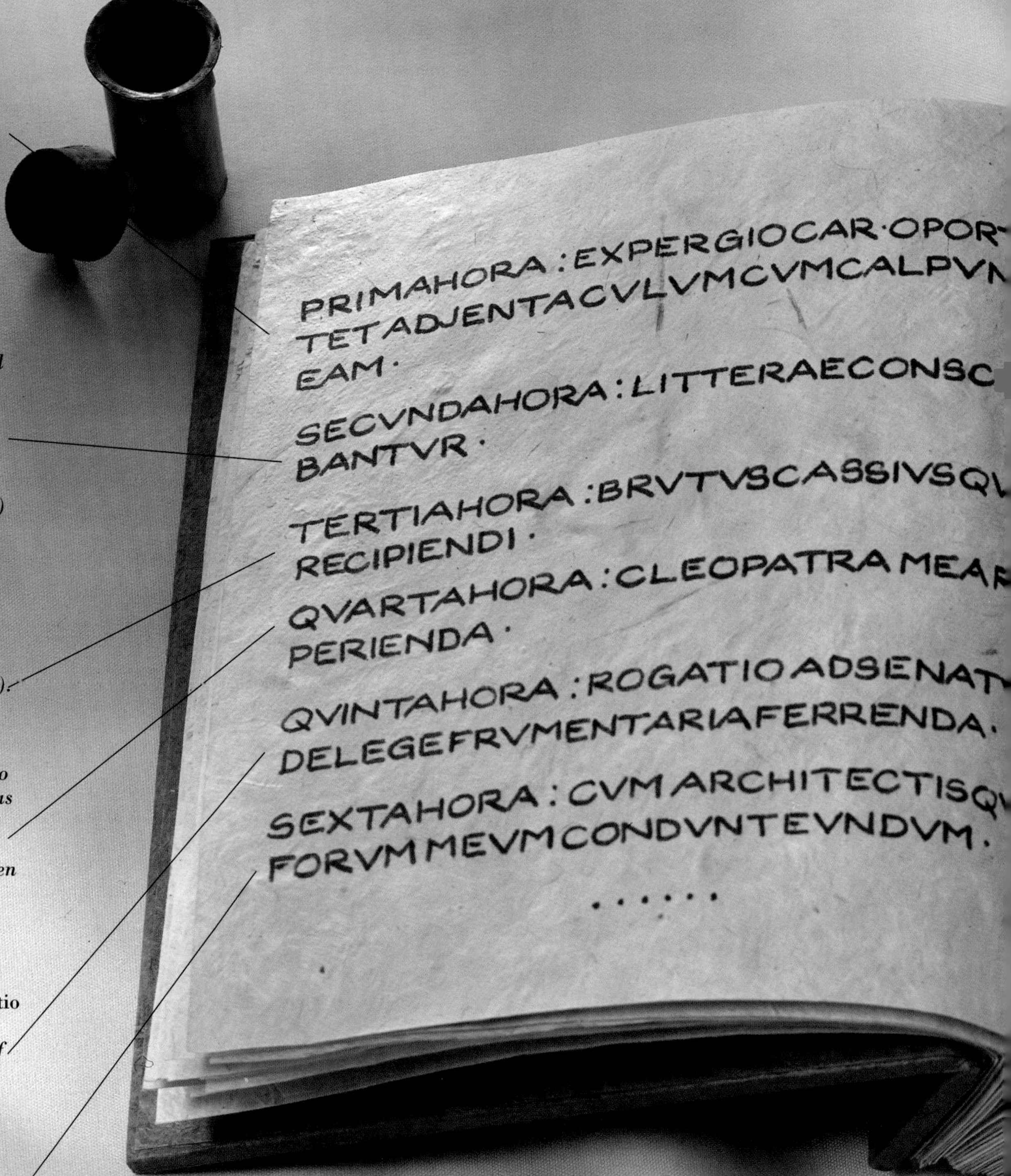
PRIMAHORA : EXPERGIOCAR · OPOR
TETADJENTACVLVMCVMCALPVN
EAM ·
SECVNDAHORA : LITTERAECONSC
BANTVR ·
TERTIAHORA : BRVTVSCASSIVSQV
RECIPIENDI ·
QVARTAHORA : CLEOPATRA MEAR
PERIENDA ·
QVINTAHORA : ROGATIO ADSENAT
DELEGEFRVMENTARIAFERRENDA ·
SEXTAHORA : CVM ARCHITECTISQV
FORVMMEVMCONDVNTEVNDVM ·
· · · · · ·

Conversation, honors, laws, triumphs
Here's the jam-packed agenda for

FOR A WARRIOR

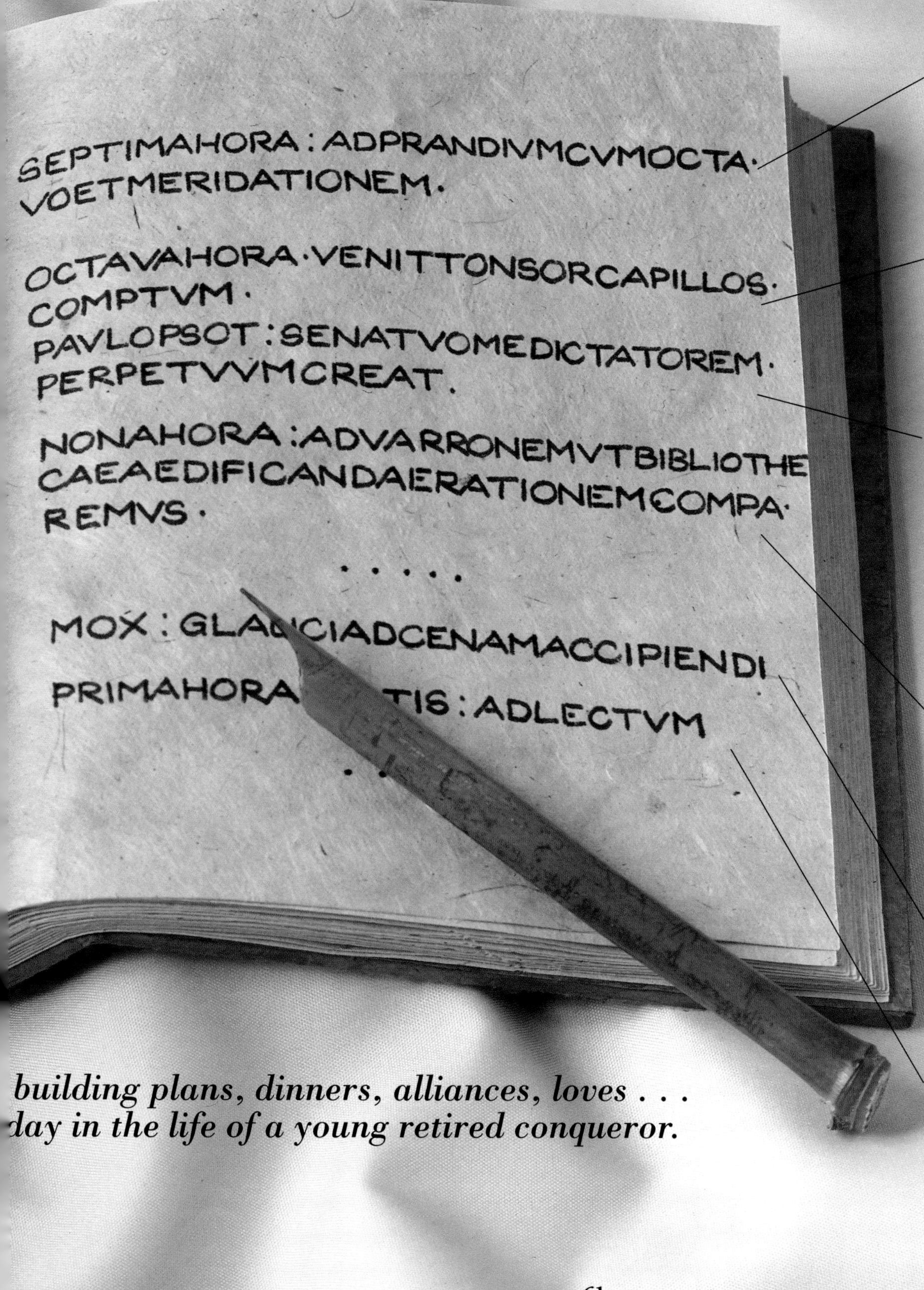
SEPTIMAHORA : ADPRANDIVMCVMOCTA·
VOETMERIDATIONEM·
OCTAVAHORA·VENITTONSORCAPILLOS·
COMPTVM·
PAVLOPSOT : SENATVOMEDICTATOREM·
PERPETVVMCREAT·
NONAHORA : ADVARRONEMVTBIBLIOTHE
CAEAEDIFICANDAERATIONEMCOMPA·
REMVS·
MOX : GLA CIADCENAMACCIPIENDI
PRIMAHORA TIS : ADLECTVM

12:00: Prantium *(light lunch consisting of cold meat and fruit) with Octav (his grand-nephew whom he adopts because he has no male heir).*

1:00: Visit from the tonsor *("barber").*

1:30: The senate to give me the title of dictator for life. (The republic is on the edge of the abyss. By now, all the democratic institutions, while still maintained, are completely devoid of meaning.)

2:00: See Varro about the plans for my public library (the first in Italy).

2:30: The Glaucuses are coming to dinner. (The convivium, *which is divided into three parts:* gustatio, *or appetizer;* prima mensa, *or first course; and* secunda mensa, *or second course.)*

8:00 (6:00 in winter): To bed!

building plans, dinners, alliances, loves . . .
day in the life of a young retired conqueror.

I, MARCELLUS C., 30 YEARS OLD, ROMAN CITIZEN

Every summer morning I rise at 4:30 a.m. with the sun (7:30 in the winter). After splashing a little water on my arms and legs I'm ready to start the day. Next it's a *jentaculum* of bread, cheese, and fruit. From 9:00 to 10:00 I see my clients (I'm a lawyer), then I go to the Rostra, the platform for haranguing, to make a speech for the defense in some corruption case. Another day, another corruption case!

Rome has changed now that Caesar is in charge. There's construction all over the place—it's making it harder and harder to get anywhere. And you can't take a step in any direction without coming nose to nose with a new statue of the dictator.

A little while ago, I heard rumors at the Forum that Caesar wants to become king. Even if he does, he knows very well that the idea of a monarchy is taboo around here. Since the fall of the Tarquin kings (509 B.C.), nobody wants to hear about it anymore. The citizens have only one word on their lips—"democracy"—and yet those who are in power do more to advance their own causes than those of the people. Allow me to quote Cicero: "It was by the votes of the rich, not the poor, that all was decided."

Ugh, what a stench! In the middle of July the air is unbearable. Fortunately, I always take along my ball of ambergris to rub on my hands.

After my case, I'll go to the *tonsor* to get my hair cut and curled. Alexandrus is the best: he makes my hair smell great, pulls out my nose hairs (I would get my arms done, too, but I don't have the time), gives me a manicure, all for only three sesterces! Marcia asked me to bring home some fish, and I hope I don't forget. Shopping at the Forum is really convenient; you can find anything there!

At noon, Marcia makes me a light meal (*prantium*)—cold meat, fruit, a glass of wine—after which I'll take a little nap.

Later, I'll meet up with my friends at the Forum, but I can't spend too much time because we're having guests for dinner at 2:30, and it looks like it's going to be a long evening.

On the *convivium* (dinner) menu: *gustatio*, or appetizer, of honeyed wine, hard-boiled eggs, and olives; then *prima mensa*, or first course, of fish (turbot) or meat (wild boar, chicken); then sweets, then the *secunda mensa*, or second course, of shellfish, fruit, and honeycakes. As far as drinks go, it will be wine mixed with water.

CITY MEDICINE

The first "family doctors" came to Rome from Greece at the end of the third century B.C. Many doctors are slaves or freedmen. They see patients in their offices, which are set up inside little shops, or make house calls. The fees are on a sliding-scale basis. Although dissection of cadavers and animals is widely practiced, medical knowledge is still quite limited. The first private medical school is established at the beginning of the first century B.C.

Specialists appear a century later: surgeons (also known as "wound doctors"), eye doctors (there are many of them), and dentists. Herbal medicine utilizing such plants as sage and rosemary is also popular.

Apothecaries, or "drug sellers," sell medicinal plants as well as miracle potions for dyeing the hair or making it grow. Traveling charlatans abound. Caesar grants doctors—Greeks, mostly—the right to establish themselves within the city.

In an earlier time, Cato the Censor (234-149 B.C.), great-grandfather of Cato of Utica, was known for being fervently anti-Greek. In his time, all the doctors are Greek. Moreover, he finds it scandalous that doctors charge their patients. He did not appreciate the standard treatment of the Greek doctors. Here are some of the cures he put in his treatise on medicine, after testing them out on members of his family:

- for digestive problems, sleeplessness, diseases of the eye, sores, ulcers, and headaches: cabbage, the miracle vegetable of a thousand uses.
- for colic: a good pomegranate decoction.
- for sciatica: juniper wood wine.
- kind words or music are just as good a remedy!

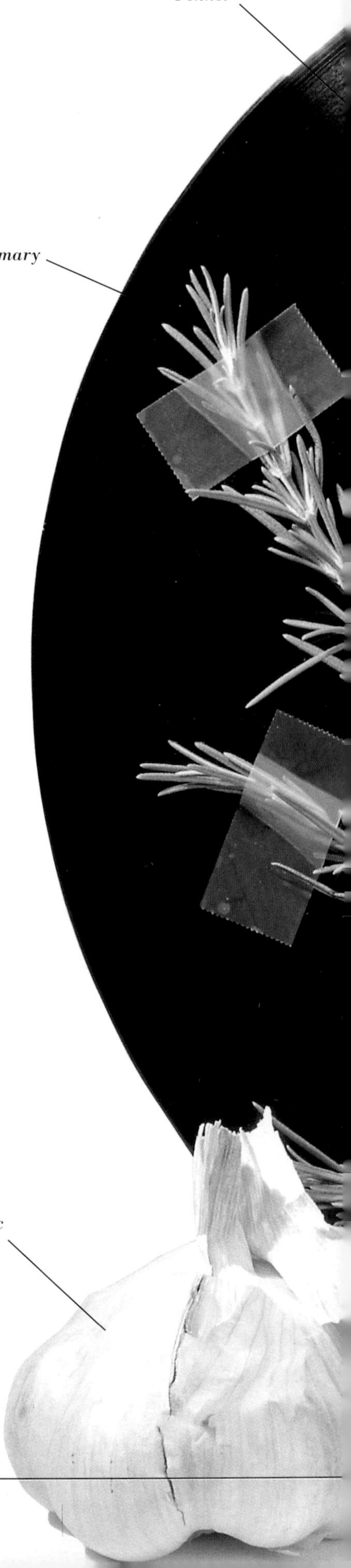
Fennel
Rosemary
Garlic
Mustard seed

Words and music
Sage
Cabbage

DIVO·VESPASIANO AVGVSTO
TI·CAESAR·AVG·D·AVGVSTI·F·
D·IVLI·N·OB·RECEPTA·SIGNA·
CVM·VARO·AMISSA·DVT·V·
TI·GERMANIS·CAESAR·

CAESAR'S BIG

"The limits of the foreign territories are well defined, those of the city of Rome are those of the world." (Ovid) In spite of its marshy site, Rome has an exceptional location. The city is surrounded by seven hills (the Capitoline, Quirinal, Viminal, Esquiline, Caelian, Aventine, and Palatine), which protect it, the Tiber River borders it on the west, and it is only 16 *milles*[1] from the Tyrrhenian Sea. Rome possesses a virtual sacred boundary, the *pomerium*, which all armed persons are forbidden to cross, as well as the 3,800-foot stone Servian Walls built under the sixth king of Rome, Servius Tullius (570-534 B.C.). Rome has been built and rebuilt without a plan. In such a labyrinth, Romans use monuments to find their way around because the streets have no names. Each quarter, often consisting of a single street, has its specialty: books and courtesans in the Tuscan quarter, leather in Argiletum, prostitutes and taverns in Subura (where Caesar grew up). The streets are winding, and big avenues, called *via*, sometimes up to 20 feet wide, are rare. The most beautiful temple of Caesar's era, the temple of Jupiter, is on the Capitoline Hill. Founded in 509 B.C., it has a roof tiled in bronze and has the distinction of having a triple sanctuary honoring Jupiter, Juno, and Minerva. Most temples in Rome are rectangular. They are always built in honor of a particular deity, a statue of whom can be found in the *cella*, or main room. There are no windows; only the doorway lets in light. The temple is a place of worship, but can also serve as a meeting place for the senate. The Curia, the senate's usual meeting place, is in the Forum. When it burns down in 52 B.C. Caesar orders its reconstruction. The Theater of Pompey, erected in 55 B.C., is the first semicircular theater built of stone and has tiers (earlier theaters were built of wood, and the audience stood). Romans enjoy the

PROJECTS

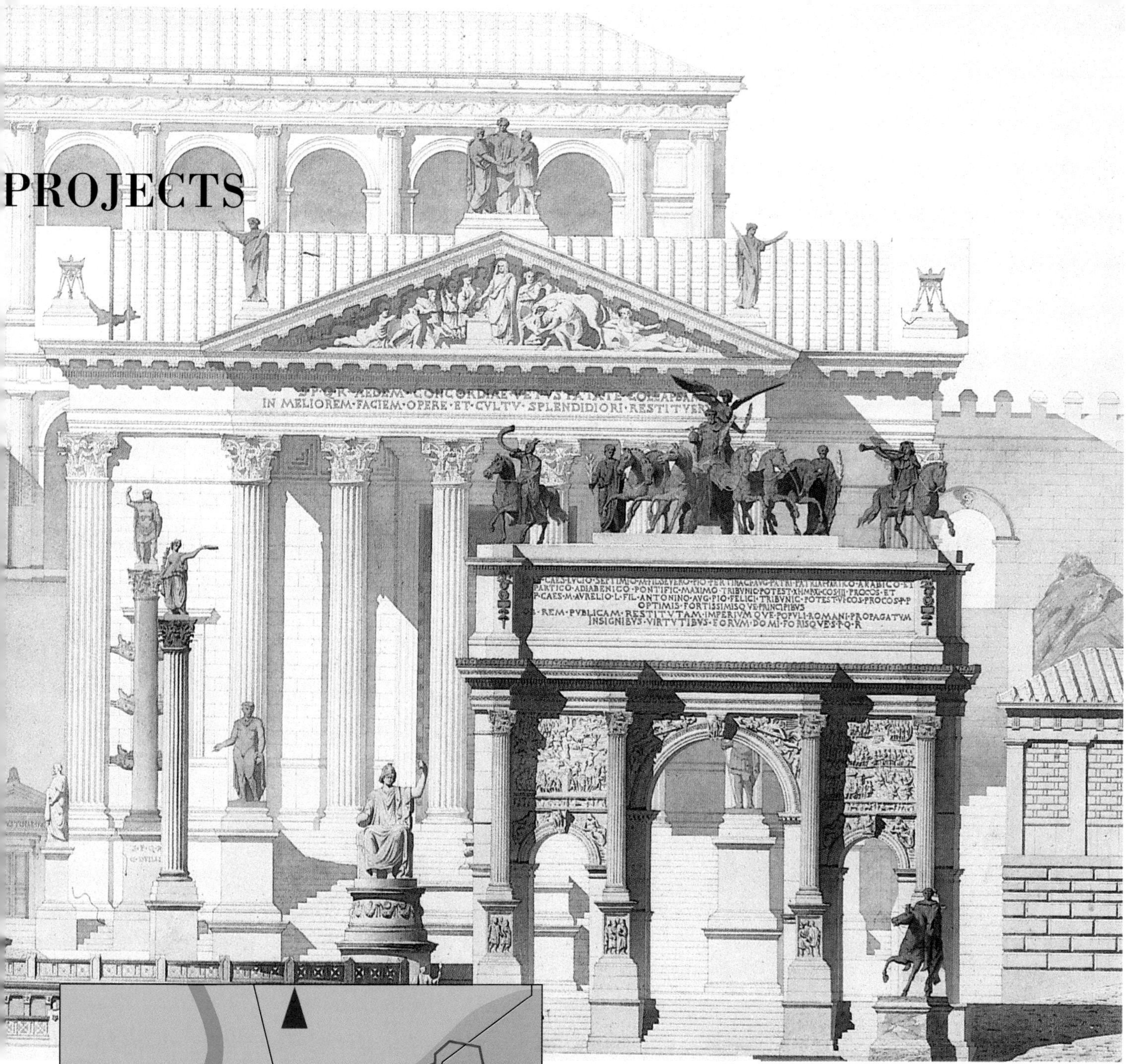

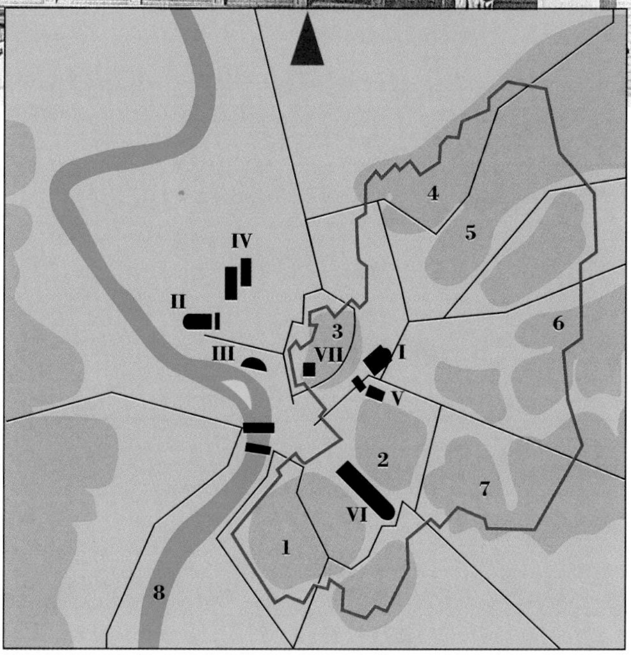
IV
II
III
I
VII
3
V
4
5
6
2
7
VI
1
8

1. Aventine. 2. Palatine. 3. Capitoline. 4. Quirinal. 5. Viminal. 6. Esquiline. 7. Caelian. 8. Tiber River.
I. Forum. II. Theater of Pompey. III. Theater of Marcellus. IV. Saepta Iulia. V. Temple of Venus. VI. Circus Maximus. VII. Temple of Jupiter.

theater, but are not fanatics. Caesar wants to make his hometown bigger and more airy. He has an intense interest in architecture and urban planning; once he comes to power, he throws himself into big projects. In the city itself, he has construction begin on the Basilica Julia, the Forum of Julius Caesar (north of the current Forum) with its temple dedicated to Venus Genetrix[2], his alleged ancestor, and the first public library. He has the Curia face in a new direction, wants to put down new flagstone in the Forum, and undertakes the construction of a large theater (the Marcellus). He has the Rostra moved. He wants to build a new Campus Martius. He also wants to divert the Tiber, enlarge the port of Ostia, and dry up the Pontine Marshes. So many projects, so little time!

1. One *mille* = a thousand Roman steps, or approximately 1,500 feet.
2. He swore that if he won the battle at Pharsalus, he would build this temple. He won the battle and kept his promise.

ROMAN ART, OR IMITATION IS

Roman art itself was born around 100 B.C., coinciding with the conquest of Greece. The Roman conquerors widely looted Greece of its magnificent art works. Italian temples, porticoes, basilicas, and columns all show the Greek influence. Over the centuries, basilicas evolved into courts of law. At first, this vast hall divided into several naves was used mainly to shelter Roman citizens from the rain. The triumphal arch, a typically Roman monument, develops after Caesar's time. One very famous arch is that of the emperor Septimius Severus (A.D. 193-211).

Mosaics arrive from Greece and remain in black and white until the end of the republic. The Romans perfect the art of the mosaic under the empire. Glassmaking develops during the first century B.C. Vases and bowls are made of cut or blown glass. Roman portraiture also dates to the end of the republican period. The realistic nature of the por-

THE SINCEREST FORM OF FLATTERY

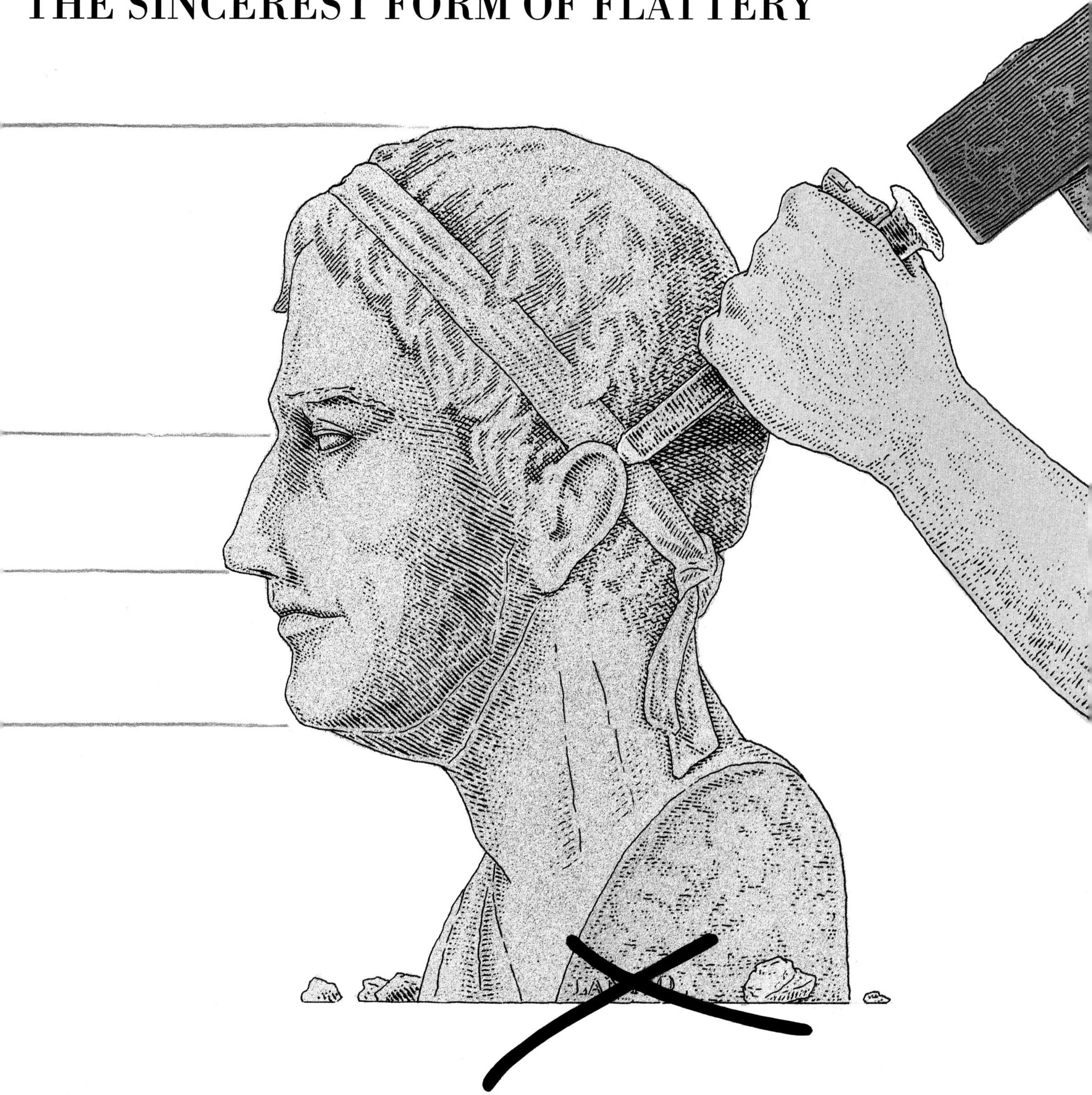

traits makes one suspect that the artists used funerary masks (*imago*[1]) for models. A few statues remain from this period; they are similar in style to Greek ones. One difference between Greek and Roman artists: the Greeks always sign their works, which is not always the case with the Romans.

The Romans love art. Cicero, a major art collector, writes to his best friend Atticus[2] in Athens, who recommends artists to him and sends him sculptures to decorate his villas, or country estates, of which he has no fewer than eight!

1. Imago: elected officials kept the funerary masks of family members in cabinets.
2. Extract from letter from Cicero to Atticus: "I love those Hermes in Pentelic marble with the bronze heads. Please send them to me A.S.A.P., along with some more statues and objets d'art."

ROME, SWEET HOME

Triclinium
Garden
Kitchen

Rome's poorest inhabitants are crowded together in *insulae*, apartment houses up to seven stories high that have been built since the third century B.C. They have windows (without windowpanes), but no running water or heat on the individual floors. Each building has a fountain downstairs. Wealthy citizens live in private houses. Houses with atriums, or large covered courtyards with a central opening in the roof, are of simple brick construction. The dining room, or *triclinium*, contains three couches arranged in a horseshoe around a table. The maximum number of guests is nine (three per couch). Only men are allowed to recline; women and children sit on chairs. The

ERRARE
HVMANVM
EST

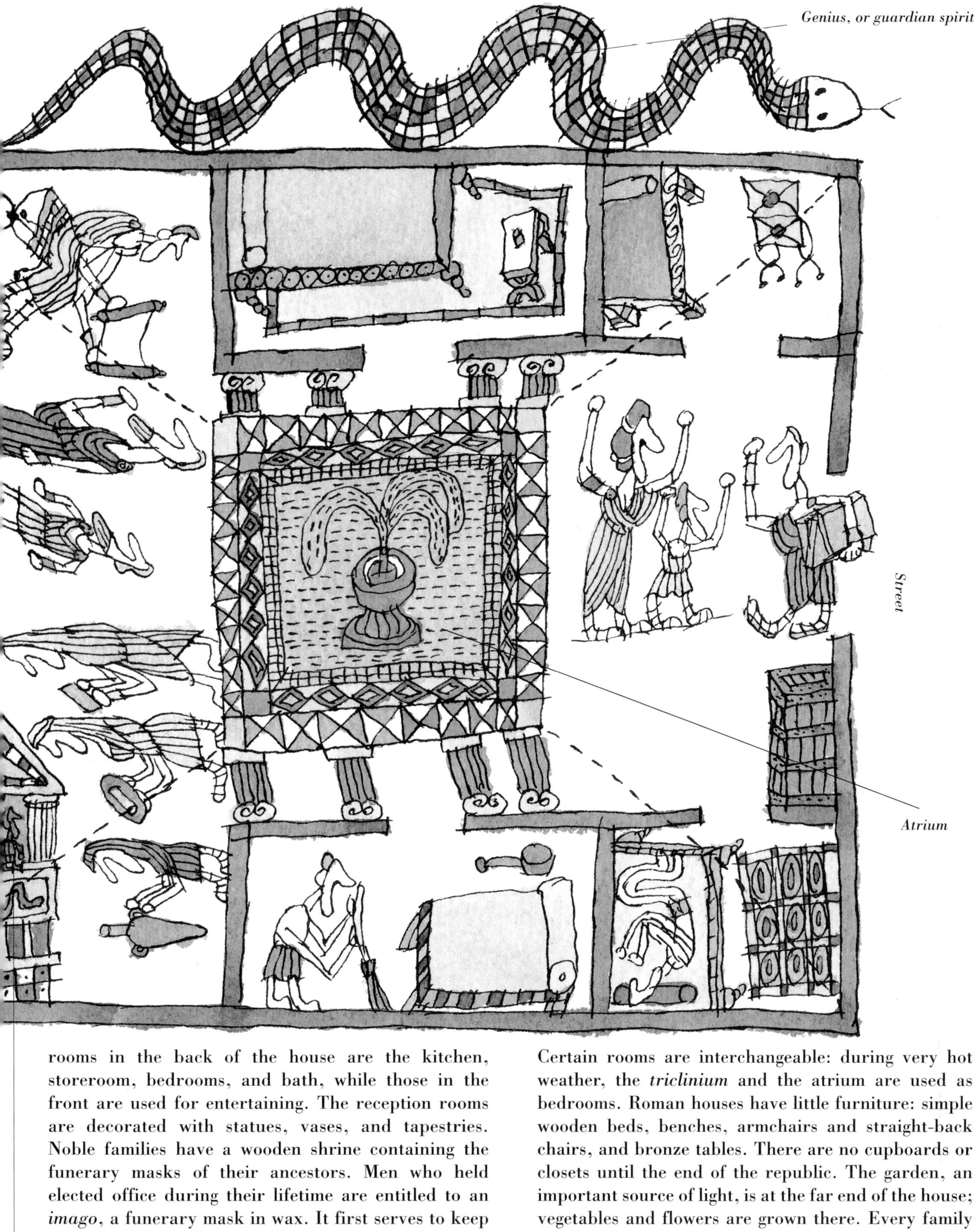
Genius, or guardian spirit
Street
Atrium

rooms in the back of the house are the kitchen, storeroom, bedrooms, and bath, while those in the front are used for entertaining. The reception rooms are decorated with statues, vases, and tapestries. Noble families have a wooden shrine containing the funerary masks of their ancestors. Men who held elected office during their lifetime are entitled to an *imago*, a funerary mask in wax. It first serves to keep the corpse from decomposing too quickly, then it is kept in a conspicuous spot in the house. The rooms are often small, and the Roman chooses the size of his atrium according to his position in society. If he is a merchant, he uses part of the atrium to house his shop.

Certain rooms are interchangeable: during very hot weather, the *triclinium* and the atrium are used as bedrooms. Roman houses have little furniture: simple wooden beds, benches, armchairs and straight-back chairs, and bronze tables. There are no cupboards or closets until the end of the republic. The garden, an important source of light, is at the far end of the house; vegetables and flowers are grown there. Every family worships three kinds of household spirits or deities: *lares*, deities that protect the household and its members, a *genius*, an ancestral guardian spirit, and *penates*, spirits of the hearth. The Romans make them offerings of fire, wine, and incense.

Lararium, or home shrine

SLAVES, DOMESTIC STYLE

(SIZE XL) . . .

There are 3 million slaves in Italy at the end of the republic. Where do they come from? Most of them are prisoners of war, or else they have been bought on the slave markets of Greece or Asia. They may also be citizens who have been stripped of their civic rights. Their status is identical to that of a woman or a child: the slave is a dependent of the head of the household. Having slaves is normal for the Romans. The wealthiest families have dozens, while most people make do with just one. In Rome, slaves are called *Satius*, "he who waits": indeed, a slave is on call twenty-four hours a day. Since he hears and sees all his master says and does, he might be tortured by those who want to get information out of him.

In general, however, slaves are well-treated, in the city as well as in the country. A slave is considered a member of the family. He plays an important role in the children's upbringing, accompanying them to school and to the market. Often, after ten or twenty years of loyal service, the master allows his slave to buy his freedom. But with what money? The master would not pay his slave for his services. Instead, the master gives him a *peculium* (literally, "small flock"), occasional small gifts of money. Once the slave is free, he does not break his ties with his former master. The latter becomes his *patronus*, "he who takes the place of a father," and continues to call him Satius in spite of his new status.

. . . AND SLAVES, WILD STYLE

(ALSO AVAILABLE IN SIZE XXL)

Domestic slaves are well treated, but such is not the case with gladiators. Who are they? Condemned Romans, slaves, and prisoners of war who live in deplorable conditions. They train for fighting in specialized schools. Gladiators are classified according to their dress and weapons: the Thracian is armed with a helmet, small round shield, and a dagger; the Samnite has a helmet, leg armor, shield, and short sword; the Gaul, or murmillone, has very little protection; and the retiarius has for his only weapons a trident and a net. During combats, two different types of gladiators are often pitted against one another. A gladiator who wins several fights might also win his freedom. The fights were introduced in Rome in 264 B.C. and quickly became very popular. In Caesar's time, they still take place at the Forum in the late afternoon. Occasionally, the slaves rebel. The revolt of Spartacus is certainly the most famous slave uprising. It takes place between 73 and 71 B.C. The leader is Spartacus, a Thracian who escapes from the gladiator school in Capua with seventy of his comrades. They are soon joined by thousands of slaves. Crassus is put in charge of subduing the revolt, and Pompey exterminates the last holdouts: he has six thousand of them crucified along the Appian Way.

ANY EXCUSE

The Roman calendar is set by the high priest and posted on the walls of the temples. Everyone is supposed to read it. Before Caesar, the calendar is lunar. It has 355 days, plus one extra month of twenty days—which gets inserted in the calendar anywhere the high priest wishes every two years—to keep in step with the solar year. The year begins in March, named for Mars, the god of war. Twelve columns divide the year, with letters for each day: F for *fastus* ("favorable") and N for *nefastus* ("unfavorable"). On N days, no political or judicial activity takes place, and it's better not to undertake anything at all, because the gods have the day off! On F days, the gods give their approval for both public and private business. Some F days are also C, or *comitial* days: the *comitia*, or assemblies, can convene. Calends (first of each month), ides (fifteenth or thirteenth), and nones (fifth or seventh) divide up the Roman calendar unequally—every month is different! Romans don't have a seven-day week yet: every nine days they are entitled to a day of rest. In 46 B.C. Caesar institutes a new calendar, the Julian calendar, still in use today with a few modifications made in the sixteenth century. It is based on the solar year, with its 365 days, plus one extra day that is inserted between February 24 and 25 every four years—the leap year. Religious holidays in honor of the gods are inscribed on the calendar. In

TO PARTY

some years, fifty days are set aside for holidays, and there are always games during those times. The aediles organize the games, but since the funds allocated by the treasury are ridiculously small compared to the expense, the aediles use money from their own pockets. The games are very costly and, being free to the public, there's no profit to be made. On the other hand, they bring in votes at election time: "Oh, yeah, I remember him, he threw us some really great games . . ." The Romans love to be entertained. The success of Epicureanism, a Greek philosophical doctrine stating that the highest good is pleasure, is proof of this. This doctrine, dating back to the third century B.C., is still very popular during Caesar's time. The Roman games (*ludi romani*), which are dedicated to Jupiter, take place during the first two weeks of September and wrap up the military season. The opening of the games is marked by a procession that crosses the city from the Campus Martius to the temple of Jupiter by way of the Forum, and ends up at the Circus Maximus, the great U-shaped arena of Rome. The sounds of flutes, citharas (lyrelike instruments), cymbals, and water organs accompany the procession, and flowers are strewn along the path. In the Circus Maximus, which holds 250,000 people, chariot races are held. Parimutuel betting (betting with odds) already exists, the difference being that the Romans bet on the charioteers, not the horses. To win, a chariot must go around the *spina* (the barrier wall down the middle of arena) as quickly as possible. Theatergoing is also part of the fun. Rome's first permanent stone theater is the Theater of Pompey, built in 55 B.C. The actors—all men—are slaves. The often intense reactions from the crowd are tempered by hired "clappers" who calm the most agitated members of the audience. Usually 20,000 spectators attend a performance.

THE CIRCUS:

"W5 ADVISES YOU THAT THIS SHOW CONTAINS GRAPHIC VIOLENCE AND MAY BE INAPPROPRIATE FOR YOUNG READERS. PARENTAL DISCRETION IS ADVISED."

Chariot races are held at the circus, with chariots drawn by two or four horses. Bets are taken on one of the four teams (the Reds, Greens, Blues, or Whites). The race consists of making seven laps around the *spina*, the barrier wall that divides the "up" stretch from the "down" stretch and prevents collisions. Other shows take place at the circus, where wild animals like

elephants (first seen in Rome in 252 B.C.) and ostriches (first Roman appearance, 197 B.C.) are displayed. Unfortunately, once they are shown to the crowd, these animals are usually brought into the arena to fight one another in cruel combats. An elephant is pitted against a panther, or several elephants against bulls, or a hippopotamus against five crocodiles (as in 58 B.C.). Romans are greedy for this kind of spectacle, which they consider, along with gladiator fights, as *munera*, or substitutes for human sacrifices, which have been forbidden since 97 B.C.

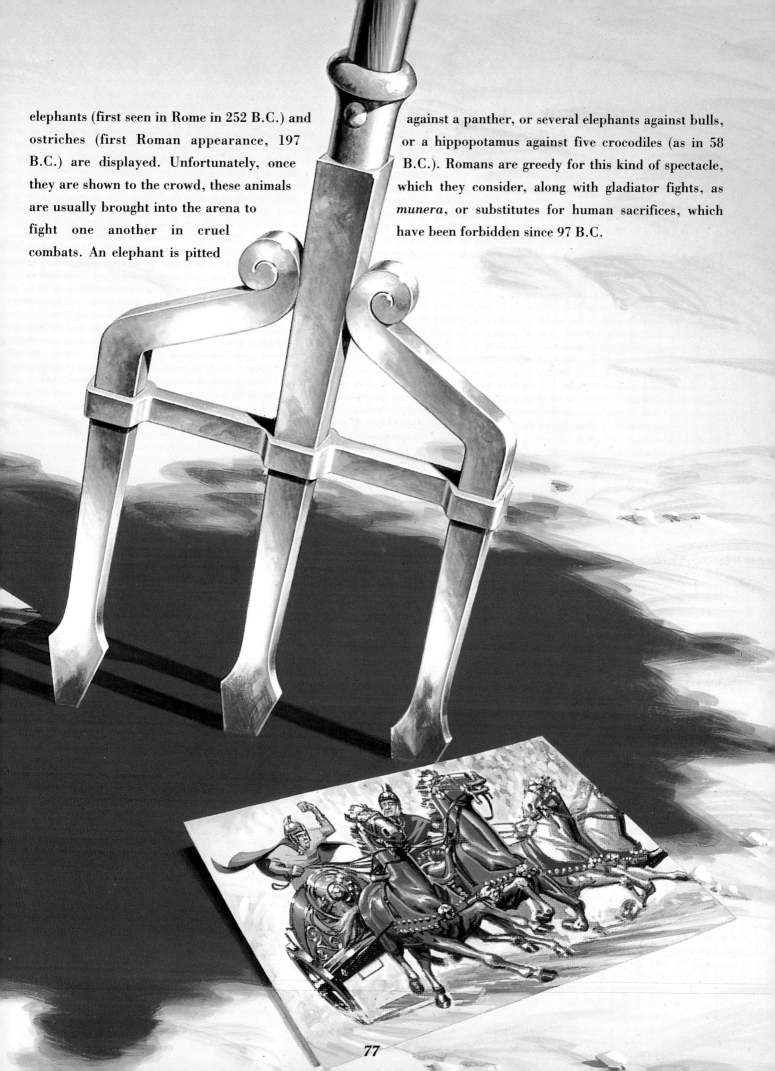

"Bread and circuses"

The Roman poet Juvenal later complains that Romans are interested only in eating (and not just bread) and chariot races in the circus. As rulers of a vast empire, the Romans have the power and means to acquire rare delicacies from all over the Mediterranean and even beyond. Most people, of course, eat simple foods, but the rich have plenty of temptations to splurge.

FAMOUS FRENCH CHEF JEAN-PIERRE COFFE DOES HIS SHOPPING IN ANCIENT ROME

For a handful of sesterces, Jean-Pierre Coffe could have brought us back kohlrabi, turnips, asparagus, mushrooms, cabbage, lettuce, onions, garlic, lentils, cucumbers, endive, and chick peas. Definitely no apricots, peaches, lemons, oranges, or melons. Too expensive? No—the Romans didn't have them yet. For a few extra sesterces, Chef Coffe, who is always telling us that our cooking is only as good as the ingredients we use, could have done like savvy Romans and gotten some top-notch veggies like leeks from Ostia and cardoons (ancestor of the artichoke) from Spain, fruit from Arpinum (Cicero's birthplace), or bass caught between the two bridges of the Tiber (near the sewers). But would he have been able to talk someone into parting with a moray from their own private saltwater-fed tank? He could always have bought some eels from the straits of Messina, oysters from Circeo, or sea urchins from Miseno, which would have been expensive enough. He would have then boiled or fried everything in oil, since butter is used only medicinally. On the sweet side, honey is used instead of sugar. And *garum*, a condiment made from fish innards mixed with salt and herbs, is used on almost everything, much as we use ketchup today. Roman gourmet cuisine, which develops at the end of the republic, is heavily influenced by Greek cooking. The famous recipe book of Apicius (that's where we got the recipes on pages 80-81) dates to the time of Augustus, more than half a century later. Just like any Roman of the time, you would be crazy about sow's udders! People started eating beef in the second century B.C.—until then cattle were considered more useful working in the fields than lying on a plate. After all, most Romans are peasants. We were thinking of giving Chef Coffe 200 sesterces, but unfortunately we don't know how much things cost back then.

1. The Trinovantes
Addedomarus
The Celts of Brittany
Gold stater
54-52 B.C.

2. Valeria
Denarius
54 B.C.

3. Nero Dupendisu
Sesterce

4. Marcus Aurelius
Bronze sesterce
A.D. 160/180

5. Junia
Head of Brutus
Denarius
54 B.C.

The Recipes of Julius Caesar

Small fish in sauce

For four people:
1 pound small fresh sardines (or other small fish such as bleak, roach, gudgeon, or sand eels)
1 1/2 ounces dried raisins
parsley
3 small white onions, minced
1 glass white wine
1 teaspoon fish stock
1 tablespoon olive oil
1 tablespoon flour

Heat the oil in a skillet. When the oil is very hot, toss in the fish and let them brown for five minutes.

In a stewpot, cook the raisins, onions, wine, fish stock, and olive oil for five minutes. Add the fish to this sauce, thicken with flour, and serve.

IN CAESAR'S TIME, ITALIANS

The Recipes of Julius Caesar

Stuffed Chicken

Stuffing:
2 parts sausage meat
1 part chopped veal
1 part chopped lamb brains
savory, parsley, cumin, salt, pepper, onions, and fresh ginger

Combine the stuffing ingredients and cook lightly in a sauté pan. Add half a glass of sweet wine.

Stuff the chicken and cook in the oven or on a rotisserie with a few strips of bacon.

Cut in half and serve.

The Recipes of Julius Caesar

Mock dried cod

For four people:
1 pound chicken, lamb, hare, or goat livers
pinch of pepper or salt
1 tablespoon fish stock
2 tablespoons olive oil
Cooking time: 5-10 minutes

Cook the chicken, lamb, hare, or goat livers. Grind and add pepper or salt and oil.

With a mold, your mixture will take on the shape of a fish. Before serving, drizzle olive oil on the platter.

DON'T HAVE PIZZA OR PASTA

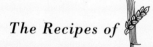

The Recipes of Julius Caesar

Honey rolls

For four people:
8 dinner rolls
1/2 liter good red wine
1 tablespoon white wine
3 pinches pepper
2 cups milk
20 whole cloves
1 teaspoon honey for each roll
1 teaspoon pepper or cumin
Cooking time: 2-3 minutes

Soak the rolls one hour in the wine, honey, and pepper. Gently squeeze out the liquid and let the rolls dry.

Soak the rolls in milk. When they have absorbed the milk, stick the cloves into them and heat them briefly in the oven, taking care not to let dry them out.

As soon as you have removed them from the oven, score the rolls and pour honey over them. Sprinkle with pepper or cumin before serving.

CAESAR AND CLEOPATRA

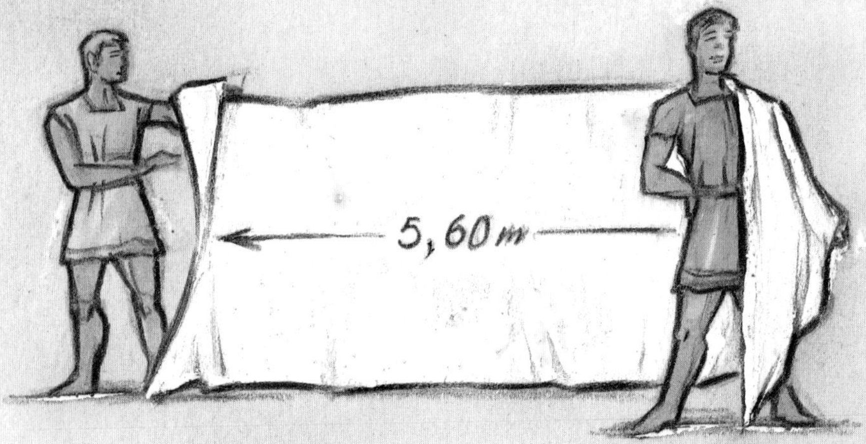
5,60 m

How to put on a toga

When we think of Roman fashion, we think of the toga. The Romans got the idea from the Etruscans, an ancient people who once inhabited central Italy. Made of thick white wool, it is the symbol of Roman citizenship. Slaves and freedmen don't have the right to wear one: their *paela*, a sleeveless coat, immediately identifies them as noncitizens. By the end of the republic, the toga has gotten longer. Roman citizens need a veritable battalion of servants to dress them, because a toga is eighteen feet long (5.6 meters) and six feet wide! The look of a toga depends on how you wrap it. Here is some advice from fashion expert Jean-Noël Robert (*Les Modes à Rome*) for doing it right: "Hold the toga lengthwise by the straight edge and gather up one-third of the material in folds. This is draped over the left shoulder. The material should hang down to the feet in front, covering the left arm and the left side of the body. The material in the back is secured with a *fibula* [clasp] on the right shoulder, so that the whole back, up to the neck, is covered. Then bring the loose end of the toga under the right arm and around to the front, draping it to about one-third of its width over the hip.

Bring the remaining material diagonally across the chest and over the left shoulder. The draping is tightened or loosened like a belt to adjust the garment."

The toga is a garment, but it can also be used to hide one's face in trying situations, literally to save face. This is what Caesar does when he is stabbed twenty-three times. Cicero wears his toga long to hide his varicose veins. He penned the famous phrase "arms yield to the toga," referring to the end of the republic, which saw military power supplanted by civil power. Men's underwear is a sleeveless wool tunic, and, in earlier times, just a loincloth. Men wear short white boots (red leather for nobles) and sandals (*solea*) with leather or ribbon lacings. Roman women wear a floor-length white tunic (*stola*), belted at the waist. Over that goes a light mantle or sleeveless coat called a *palla*. Under their tunics is the ancestor of the bra, the *strophium*. On their feet, they wear embroidered or beaded sandals. Married women wear a pleated dress, close-fitting at the waist, with an embroidered border.

GET A NEW LOOK

(or, IT'S A WRAP!)

Today, togas are no longer used for covering our bodies but our furniture. Chairs, tables, sofas, armchairs, all are artfully draped in folded fabric.

FOR KIDS FROM SEVEN TO SEVENTY-SEVEN,

Games of chance, and the betting that accompanies them, are forbidden by law, but no one pays attention.

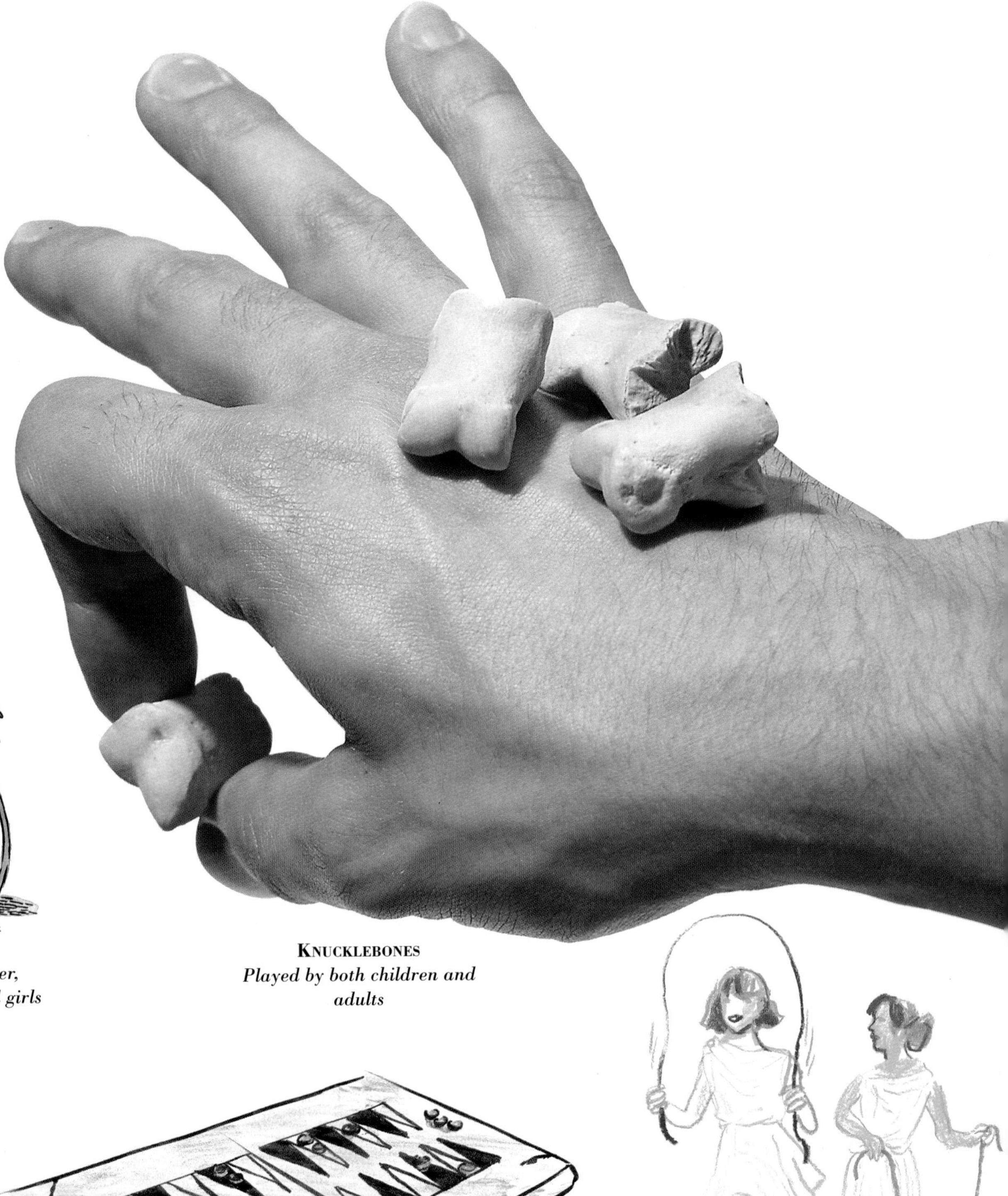

Hoops
Made of wood or copper, enjoyed by both boys and girls

Knucklebones
Played by both children and adults

Backgammon

Jump rope
Even for adults

GAMES FROM ACROSS THE CENTURIES

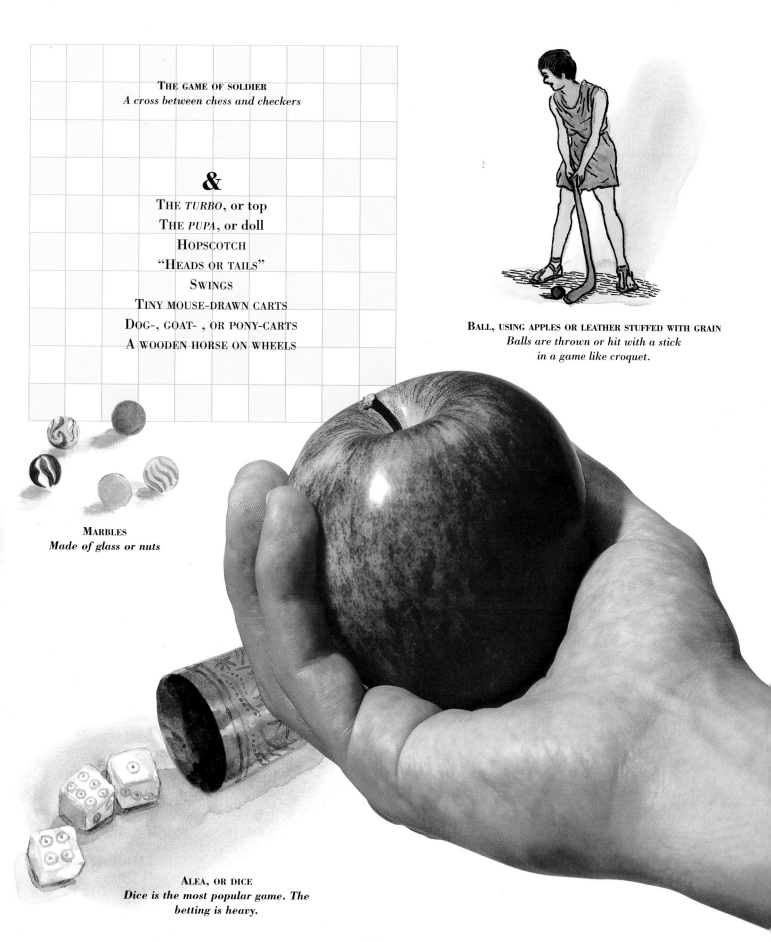

The game of soldier
A cross between chess and checkers

&

The *turbo*, or top
The *pupa*, or doll
Hopscotch
"Heads or tails"
Swings
Tiny mouse-drawn carts
Dog-, goat- , or pony-carts
A wooden horse on wheels

Ball, using apples or leather stuffed with grain
Balls are thrown or hit with a stick in a game like croquet.

Marbles
Made of glass or nuts

Alea, or dice
Dice is the most popular game. The betting is heavy.

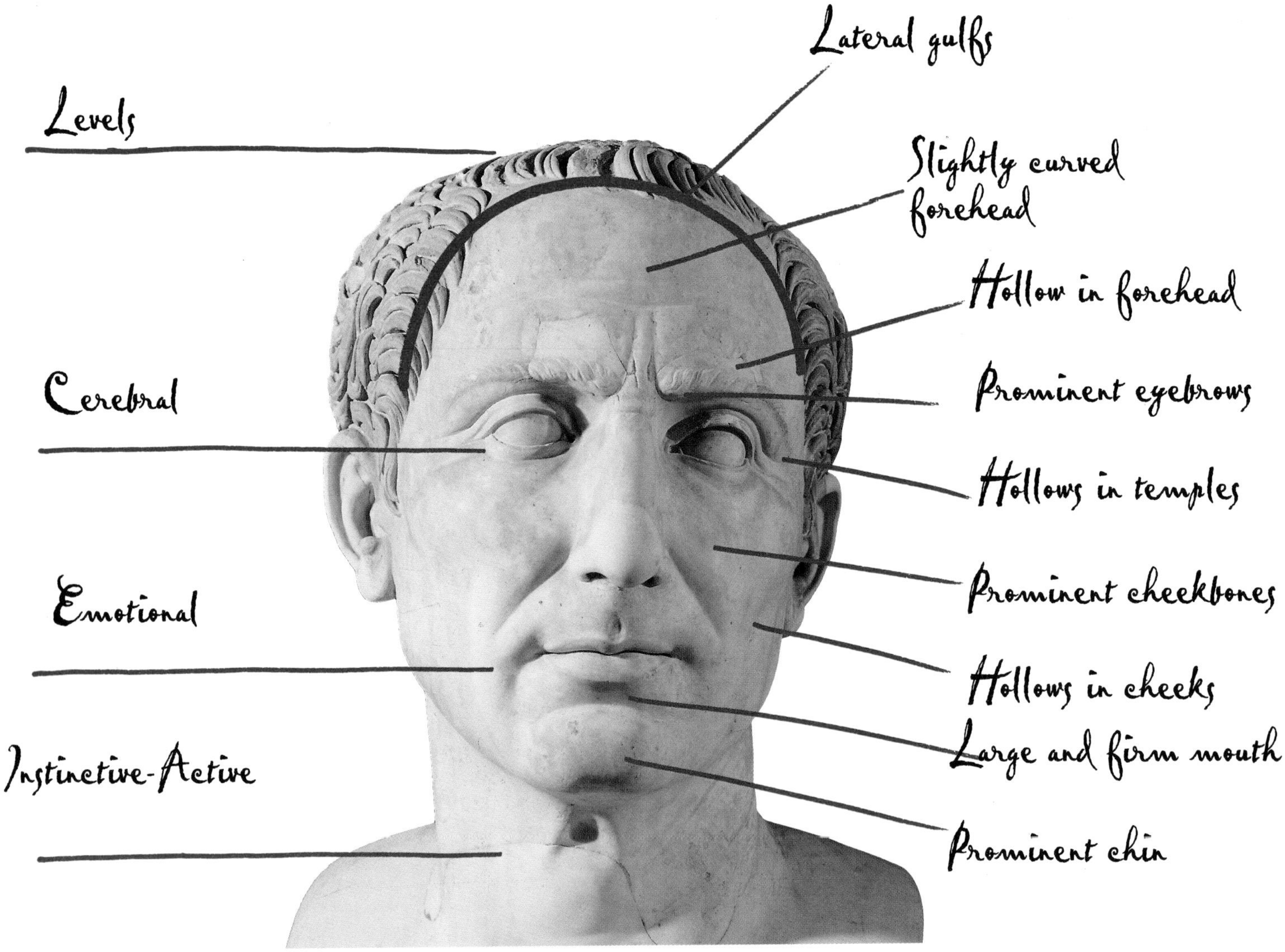
Lateral gulfs
Levels
Slightly curved forehead
Hollow in forehead
Cerebral
Prominent eyebrows
Hollows in temples
Emotional
Prominent cheekbones
Hollows in cheeks
Instinctive-Active
Large and firm mouth
Prominent chin

CAESAR: ANALYSIS
(AT AN UNUSUAL CAREER COUNSELING SERVICE)

What is immediately striking about this face is the extraordinary force it conveys. The model is marked by hollows (temples, between the nose and the cheekbones, middle of the forehead) and prominences (upper forehead, cheekbones). The opposition between these two vital movements of expansion and conservation indicates that this man is going to be marked by a profound duality. These two forces will inevitably nourish his violent passions.

It is common in this physiognomic type to see that, depending on the period in life, Mister X's behavior will either be spontaneous (prominences) or controlled (hollows).

Spontaneity must have been expressed in his youth by a revolt against the establishment and family and societal values, then, little by little, this spontaneity, tempered by self-control and maturity, became a way of life.

A hard and fast physiognomic rule is that the stronger the contrasts, the more the subject will need vital power and intellectual qualities to master them.

Cerebral level

The forehead is rather large and very differentiated, somewhat straight; it widens toward the top like a bowl due to the very compressed temples, flowing from large lateral gulfs.

The lower forehead has a different style with very prominent eyebrow bumps over somewhat deep-set eyes. There are two vertical furrows between the eyes and a break between the forehead and the nose.

Interpretation

It is immediately apparent that this is an individual of a very high intellectual level with remarkable gifts of thought, the three zones of the forehead being equally differentiated (large differentiated foreheads indicate a predisposition to genius). The field of conscience is wide (bowl), the subject has a very large capacity for synthesis, a very clear thought process, well-channeled ideas (compressed temples), and a prodigious memory. Idealism is not absent (lateral gulfs); he is a demanding perfectionist and detests vulgarity.

The upper forehead seems to indicate a strong taste for art, fine craftsmanship, and architecture—anything that satisfies his spirit. On the other hand, he is not a utopian idealist because the bumps of his lower forehead indicate a sense of the concrete and a need for the tangible and rational. Results are more important than theories. A man of duty (straight forehead, deep-set eyes, narrow temples), he is very attached to laws and he especially has a sense of service and honor.

He has exceptional ambition: if he has plans, they will be grandiose and very carefully drawn up (hollows indicate a persistent abstraction from present events).

His mouth, firm, fine, and well-defined, gives him great powers of logical formulation, order, and clarity. He must be an excellent public speaker, capable of turning a situation to his advantage, boosting a team's sagging morale or calming a rebellion.

His capacity to concentrate and his long attention span (vertical creases between the eyes) allow him to think for rather long periods of time and produce bold ideas, given his capabilities.

Emotional level

Very prominent cheekbones, conquering nose pointing forward, flaming nostrils characterize a strongly passionate man capable of the best and the worst.

However, the overall fineness, the total absence of ungainly features, combined with the power of the "frame" give him remarkable human qualities; he attaches great importance to people's esteem for him.

While the nose and cheekbones are very prominent, allowing the subject to conquer, to move ahead, to outdo himself, the hollows of the cheeks and temples allow him to reflect and also give him control.

He must be able to use his eyes, ears, and mind at the same time; that is, he must be able to listen to a counselor, give dictation, read a report, and think about the future.

One can see that this man is building his life's accomplishments with his entire being. A great seducer, seemingly capable of anything in order to achieve his goals, it is not out of the question that his spirit of conquest goes beyond the family. The strict lifestyle of his family is apparently too confining for him.

He will constantly need to be on the move and conquer. He will always want to gain ground because of his extreme ambition. He will apparently use his personal relationships to get ahead; he knows how to use others, not necessarily in an underhanded manner but rather out of the conviction that he is right. He needs to feel loved and he is not convinced that he has a lot of friends. This doesn't stop him from bending over backward for others.

Instinctive-active level

The head is well-defined, the maxillaries are prominent, the chin stands out, the mouth is large and firm.

These characteristics reveal a taste for pleasure, luxury, and refinement. When it comes to taking action, he has leadership skills; he is apparently capable of making people obey him through their sheer fascination for him. He has endless reserves of energy.

The double influence of activity on intelligence allows him to put his ideas into action and to base his activities on concepts.

The power of his spirit and clarity of his ideas are expressed with mathematical precision. Perhaps capable of blind rages that fester for long periods before exploding, he is the prototype of the man inclined to revenge.

Finally, we have to consider as an ascetic tendency his capacity for sacrificing the incidental for the overall goal, knowing that once he has given himself a goal, he apparently knows how to renounce life's pleasures. Even if he adapts to life in the present, he is very oriented toward the future (prominences), which makes him a progressive traditionalist.

Conclusion

His potential for intellect, emotion, and action channeled into abstraction, conception, and pragmatism, and enhanced by the desire for discovery, experimentation, and conquest make for an extraordinarily complete individual.

He belongs to the race of builders, of men of genius whom one meets so rarely in the career counseling business. He should go far.

THE IDES OF MARCH: CAESAR

IS ASSASSINATED

For some time now, Caesar's enemies have been trying to entrap him into saying he wants to be king. Early in 44 B.C., some citizens greet him using the title of king, to which he responds: "I am called Caesar and not king." Not a very convincing reply for a dictator[1]! On February 15, during the Lupercalian festival[2], Caesar, seated before the crowd, refuses a white crown wreathed with laurel leaves (the royal crown of the period). Three times Mark Antony, his cavalry master and a Lupercus, attempts to put the crown on his head. The people do not seem pleased, and Caesar rejects the crown. He gets the message—nobody wants him to be king.

A conspiracy is brewing, organized by Cassius and Brutus, son of Caesar's former mistress. These men are close to Caesar, so he doesn't suspect them. The night before his death, his wife, Calpurnia, has a strange dream[3] and begs Caesar not to go to the senate. He goes anyway, but is warned along the way by a "well-meaning friend." It is March 15, the ides of March. Another man warns him and slips a note into his hand, which Caesar does not read. He then meets the soothsayer who has once before told him to beware the ides of March, and who now warns him again. Caesar says: "The ides of March have come, and all is well," to which the man replies, "Yes, they have come, but they have not yet gone." When he arrives at the Curia of Pompey at 11:00 a.m., men crowd around him, as is usual for the most powerful figure in Rome. Then one of the conspirators grabs at Caesar's toga, exposing his neck. That is the signal. Caesar is stabbed twenty-three times at the foot of the statue of Pompey. Among the conspirators are some of the senators. The assassins flee, the others disperse. It is said that it was only in the evening that Caesar's slaves came to take away his body, and that the crumpled note of warning was still in his hands. He never had a chance to read it.

Calpurnia begs Caesar not to go to the senate.

1. Caesar is elected dictator—an extraordinary position granting unlimited military and political power for a period of six months—for the first time in 49 B.C. In 46 B.C., he is given the dictatorship for ten years, and in 44 B.C., for life.
2. On this occasion, young men called Luperci, members of noble families, oil their bodies and wear goatskin loincloths as they participate in an ancient purification ceremony. They race around the Palatine Hill, lashing at women with strips of goat hide to ensure fertility.
3. In Calpurnia's dream, the triumphal ornaments on the roof have been torn off by a storm. She interprets her dream as a threat to her husband's life, but she cannot convince him to stay home.

Claude
RAINS

Michel
SERRAULT

Lo
CALH

20
centuries later...

Marlon
& BRANDO
in the role of Mark Antony

Julius Caesar, along with Napoleon, is one of those political figures whose life and loves have often inspired moviemakers.
Caesar has one advantage over Napoleon: Shakespeare wrote a play about him!

uis Rex Dom

ERN HARRISON DE LUISE

Chronology of Caesar at the cinema:

1934: Cleopatra
directed by Cecil B. De Mille,
starring Claudette Colbert

1945: Caesar and Cleopatra
directed by Gabriel Pascal,
starring Vivien Leigh and Claude Rains.

1953: Julius Caesar
directed by Joseph L. Mankiewicz,
starring Marlon Brando and Louis Calhern.

1960: Spartacus
directed by Stanley Kubrick,
starring Kirk Douglas and Laurence Olivier.

1963: Cleopatra
directed by Joseph L. Mankiewicz,
starring Elizabeth Taylor and Richard Burton.

1966: A Funny Thing Happened on the Way to the Forum,
directed by Richard Lester,
starring Zero Mostel and Phil Silvers.

1970: Julius Caesar
directed by Stuart Burge,
starring Charlton Heston and Jason Robards.

1981: History of the World—Part I,
directed by Mel Brooks,
starring Mel Brooks and Dom DeLuise.

CAESAR & CO.

Get Top Billing

CAESAR IS DEAD, LONG LIVE

The funeral

A funeral pyre is readied at the Campus Martius, near the tomb of his daughter, but Caesar's body will not be taken there. Instead, he is cremated at the Forum, where his body has been lying in state. In a public show of mourning, the crowd throws weapons, jewelry, and clothing into the flames as a sign of respect.

Caesar's last will and testament

He makes Octavian, his grand-nephew and adopted son, his heir, but he leaves his gardens to the Roman people and gives each citizen 300 sesterces. In September, the cult of *Divus Julius* is established—Romans begin to worship Caesar as a god.

Funerary urn
Late second-early first century B.C.

After Caesar

Rome is in an uproar. The assassins flee and are not beaten by Mark Antony and Octavian until 42 B.C. in the battle of Philippi, in Macedonia. Then the two victors engage in their own power struggle for succession. Octavian wins the battle of Actium in September 31 B.C. against Mark Antony's fleet and becomes the new master of Rome. He is the first Roman emperor and uses the title Augustus. Napoleon wrote: "Once Caesar was dead, he was replaced by Antony, by Octavian, by Tiberius, by Nero, and, after the latter, all human combinations were played out for six hundred years." All future Roman emperors will take the title "Caesar," and the word will be adopted in other languages: *kaiser* (German) and *czar* (Russian).

THE CAESARS

Augustus
27 B.C.-A.D. 14

Tiberius
A.D. 14-37

Caligula
37-41

Claudius
41-54

Nero
54-68

Vespasian
69-79

Titus
79-81

Domitian
81-96

Nerva
96-98

Trajan
98-117

Hadrian
117-138

Antoninus Pius
138-161

Marcus Aurelius
161-180

Commodus
180-192

Septimius Severus
193-211

Caracalla
211-217

Nero

Tiberius

Trajan

Claudius

Titus

Hadrian

Caracalla

Augustus

100-44 B.C.

- **EXIST**
- **DON'T EXIST YET**

I
II
III
IV
V
VI
VII
VIII
IX

es (to eat) XII. Carrier pigeons XIII.
) X. Hats (although freedmen wore a
r) XV. Mosaics in color XVI. Potatoes

CDROME

X
XI
XII
XIII
XIV
XV
XVI
XVII
XVIII

EXIST: I. Bras II. Seven-story apartment buildings IV. Graffiti V. Dentures VII. House slippers IX. Pink fla
Aqueducts (since the Appia, 312 B.C.) XVII. Curling irons XVIII. Tourist guides
DON'T EXIST YET: III. Pizza. VI. Thermal baths VIII. The Colosseum (built by the emperor Titus in A.
cone-shaped bonnet) XI. Cookbooks (the first is by Apicius, under Augustus) XIV. Sugar (honey was used as a swe

INDEX

BOOKS FOR FURTHER READING

Apicius. *Cookery and Dining in Imperial Rome*. Trans. by Joseph D. Vehling. New York: Dover, 1977.

Boardman, John; Griffin, Jasper; Murray, Oswyn. *The Oxford History of the Roman World*. Oxford: Oxford University Press, 1991.

Burrell, Roy, and Connolly, Peter. *The Romans*. Oxford: Oxford University Press, 1991.

Caesar, Julius. *The Civil War*. Trans. by Jane F. Mitchell. Harmondsworth: Penguin Books, 1980.

———. *The Conquest of Gaul*. Trans. by S. A. Handford, revised by Jane F. Gardner. Harmondsworth: Penguin Books, 1982.

Carcopino, Jérôme. *Daily Life in Ancient Rome*. Trans. by E. O. Lorimer. New Haven and London: Yale University Press, 1968.

Cicero, Marcus Tullius. *Selected Political Speeches*. Trans. by Michael Grant. New York: Penguin Books, 1977.

Connolly, Peter. *The Legionary*. Oxford: Oxford University Press, 1990.

Coolidge, Olivia. *Caesar's Gallic War*. North Haven: Shoe String Press, 1991.

Fuller, J. F. *Julius Caesar: Man, Soldier, and Tyrant*. New York: Da Capo Press, 1991.

Nardo, Don. *Greek and Roman Theater*. San Diego: Lucent Books, 1995.

Plutarch. *The Lives of the Noble Grecians and Romans*. Trans. by John Dryden, edited and revised by Hugh Arthur Clough. 2 vols. New York: Modern Library, 1992.

Radice, Betty. *Who's Who in the Ancient World*. New York: Penguin Books, 1973.

Shakespeare, William. *Julius Caesar*. New York: Bantam, 1988.

Simon, James. *Ancient Rome*. Eyewitness Books. New York: Knopf, 1990.

Suetonius. *The Twelve Caesars*. Trans. by Robert Graves. New York: Penguin Books, 1980.

ILLUSTRATIONS

Daniel Bechenec: 40-41, 76-77
Jean-Paul Colbus: 8-9, 34-35
Philippe Convain: 82
Christian Duchesne: 94-95 (PAO)
© 1995, Éditions Albert René/Goscinny-Uderzo: 58-59
Jérôme Festy: 50-51
Gabriel Feat: cover (PAO)
Benoît Jacques: 70-71
Claude Meunier: 16-17, 48-49, 66-67, 94-95
Gérard Nicolas: 18-19, 52-53, 74-75, 84-85
Poncet de la Grave: 32-33, 68-69, 72-73
Long Tran: 38-39, 42-43
Weber: 13, 14, 24-25

PHOTO CREDITS

© Artephot: 93
© Ciné Plus: 90-91
Explorer: 54-55
© École nationale des beaux-arts: 16-17, 66-67
Jean-Blaise Hall: 80-81
Giraudon: cover, 6, 10-11, 15, 26, 28, 44-45, 55, 56-57, 86, 88-89, 93
© Jacana: 11
Philippe Jumin: 46-47, 48-49, 50-51, 64-65, 78-79, 83
Peter Lipmann: 7, 12, 20-21, 36-37
Peter Knapp: 30
Julien Poncet de la Grave: special effects 36-37
© Photo RMN: 92
Roger-Viollet: 10-11, 39, 43, 88-89
Jean-Marie Troude: 4-5, 22-23, 26-27, 60-61, 62-63, 84-85
Photos DR: 90-91
Barbara Guarnéri: designer, 80-81